ON HISTORY

a treatise

To —

Please enjoy the book —

ON HISTORY
a treatise

MARK ALBERTSON

Tate Publishing & Enterprises

On History: A Treatise
Copyright © 2009 by Mark Albertson. All rights reserved.

No part of this publication may be reproduced, stored in a retrieval system or transmitted in any way by any means, electronic, mechanical, photocopy, recording or otherwise without the prior permission of the author except as provided by USA copyright law.

The opinions expressed by the author are not necessarily those of Tate Publishing, LLC.

Published by Tate Publishing & Enterprises, LLC
127 E. Trade Center Terrace | Mustang, Oklahoma 73064 USA
1.888.361.9473 | www.tatepublishing.com

Tate Publishing is committed to excellence in the publishing industry. The company reflects the philosophy established by the founders, based on Psalm 68:11,
"The Lord gave the word and great was the company of those who published it."

Book design copyright © 2008 by Tate Publishing, LLC. All rights reserved.
Cover Design by Janae Glass
Interior design by Kandi Evans

Published in the United States of America

ISBN: 978-1-60604-689-0
1. History
2. Study & Teaching
08.11.21

Dedication

To the American people; may they take the time to heed the lessons of history, and in so doing, reverse their lack of fealty and wisdom, to recognize, root out, and then thwart the forces of greed, arrogance, and opportunism that are pledged to the destruction of our Republic.

Notable Quotes that Denote the Theme of This Work

"Here's to plain speaking and clear understanding." **Kasper Gutman to Sam Spade, The Maltese Falcon**

"Let the people know the truth, and the country is safe." **Abraham Lincoln**

"Those who begin coercive elimination of dissent soon find themselves exterminating dissenters. Compulsory unification of opinion achieves only the unanimity of the graveyard." **Felix Frankfurter**

"Our liberty depends on the freedom of the press, and that cannot be limited without being lost." **Thomas Jefferson**

"Censorship reflects a society's lack of confidence in itself." **Potter Stewart**

"There is no subtler, no surer means of overturning the existing basis of society than to debauch the currency. The process engages all the hidden forces of economic law on the side of destruction, and does it in a manner which not one man in a million is able to diagnose." **John Maynard Keynes**

"There is no nation on earth powerful enough to accomplish our overthrow.... Our destruction, should it come at all, will be from another quarter. From the inattention of the people to the concerns of their government, from their carelessness and negligence. I fear that they may place too implicit a confidence in their public servants, and fail properly to scrutinize their conduct, that in this way they may be made the dupes of designing men, and become the instruments of their undoing." **Daniel Webster**

"Human history does not lie, people do." **Mark Albertson**

"Only the suppressed word is dangerous." **Ludwig Borne**

"In years hence and after all is said and done, history will not say that in 2003, Iraq attacked the United States." **Mark Albertson**

"National hatred is something peculiar. You will always find it strongest and most violent when there is the lowest degree of culture." **Johann Wolfgang von Goethe**

"Freedom will cure most things…" **Summerhill by A. S. Neill**

"I helped make Mexico, especially Tampico, safe for American oil interests in 1914. I helped make Haiti and Cuba a decent place for the National City Bank boys to collect revenues in. I helped in the raping of half a dozen Central American republics for the benefits of Wall Street. The record of racketeering is long. I helped purify Nicaragua for the international banking house of Brown Brothers in 1909–1912. I brought light to the Dominican Republic for American sugar interests in 1916. In China I helped to see to it that Standard Oil went its way unmolested." **Brigadier General Smedley Darlington Butler, War is a Racket**

"Beware the leader who bangs the drums of war in order to whip the citizenry into a patriotic fervor, for patriotism is indeed a double-edged sword. It both emboldens the blood, just as it narrows the mind. And when the drums of war have reached fever pitch and the blood boils with hate and the mind has closed, the leader will have no need of seizing the rights of the citizenry. Rather, the citizenry, infused with fear and blinded with patriotism, will offer up all their rights unto the leader, and gladly so. How do I know? For this is what I have done. And I am Caesar!"

Table of Contents

Introduction	13
Chapter 1: *Legacy of the Little Red Schoolhouse*	23
Chapter 2: *Swing Power*	31
Chapter 3: *Killers in the White Coats*	43
Chapter 4: *Genzai Bakudan*	55
Chapter 5: *Casus Belli*	71
Chapter 6: *Decisive Front*	91
Chapter 7: *America or Amerika*	109
Sources & Postscript	123

Introduction

"The receptivity of the great masses is very limited, their intelligence is small, but their power of forgetting is enormous."

The writer? Adolf Hitler. The passage is from *Mein Kampf*, the National Socialist bible of bigotry, oppression, despotism, and conquest. A blueprint for the subjugation of not only a nation, but a continent. Yet the Third Reich the author built to last a thousand years died miserably after only twelve. But in that time, Adolf Hitler did by force of arms what Maastricht later intended in paper. His program of ethnic cleansing was of such industriousness and thoroughness that today's practitioners seem little better than amateurs of the utmost crudity. His *Geheime Stattspolizei* (the dreaded Gestapo) served as a blueprint for many a post-World War II security service. The suffering and death and horror perpetrated by the swastika and the jackboot will be an inerasable stain on the record of human history for generations to come. Perhaps this is what is meant by the Thousand-Year Reich.

Adolf Hitler remains one of history's most frightfully interesting characters. He was the first politician to campaign by airplane. His speeches and methods of propaganda have been analyzed by public speakers, advertisers, and politicians the world over. Like Napoleon, he had a photographic memory. He was a strict vegetarian and did not become a German citizen until 1932. With the utmost Austrian courtesy, he would kiss the hand of any woman he was introduced to; and yet in the same breath he could order the extermination of millions of Jews, gypsies, Slavs, and other so-called *untermensch*. As a military strategist, Hitler did show signs of sheer brilliance, such as outflanking the Maginot Line by sending his panzers through the impenetrable Ardennes; and yet he could make bonehead plays like allowing the British to escape the trap he had set for them on the beaches at Dunkirk.

The name Adolf Hitler is synonymous with torture, brutality, and murder. But beyond that, it symbolizes a national forfeiture of democratic ideals and high cultural and societal standards, when a people prostitute their faith in themselves to indulge their need for a hero, a larger-than-life figure who will lead them into Valhalla. Like the Italians used to say about Mussolini, Hitler even made the trains run on time.

Yet like *Il Duce, Der Fuhrer* proved painfully fallible in the end. The pontificate of the Teutonic ideal, the absolute who captured the loyalty of the *Wehrmacht* to himself in lieu of Germany, the unassuming Austrian with the comical, Chaplin-esque appearance who seemed to send women swooning (four committed suicide over him), a modern-day deity of hatred who was everything to some and in the end was nothing to all, is a warning sign for those ready to follow the teachings of a false prophet.

But the capacity of the masses to repeat the mistakes of history is not due solely to memory lapse. There is also the factor of deception. For in this case, history does not lie, people do. Take the case of Georgi Zhukov. General Zhukov was one of the most brilliant military minds in the twentieth century. He deserves much of the credit for the defeat of the Nazi armies on the most important land front in World War II. Yet after the war, his role in the Soviet war effort was all but minimized. He disappeared from postwar Soviet histories, and his images and photographs were expunged. Comrade Stalin was the real hero of the Great Patriotic War and its one true hero. It was because of the generalissimo's genius and love for the Motherland which, more than any other factor, brought on the defeat of the Fascist invaders. Stalin's unscrupulous distrust of any threat, real or imagined, caused thousands of followers to be reduced in stature or worse so that his position could remain secure. One of his ways of doing this was by attempting to deceive the masses by altering history. That Zhukov's brilliant generalship helped save the Soviet Union in its darkest hour is beyond question. Yet because of the Soviet penchant for secrecy and Stalin's recasting of events for personal gain, Zhukov, a highly successful commander in the greatest land war in history, never attained the popularity of a MacArthur, Patton, Montgomery, or Rommel. Yet he was, at the very least, their equal.

Treading on the heels of deception is the misconception of events. The misconception of events can cause the improper or inaccurate analysis of history. The Allied invasion of Normandy on June 6, 1944, is a case in point. The popular notion of the largest amphibious operation in history was that it was the opening of the long-awaited second front in Europe. It was the beginning of the great rollback of the Nazi armies in France and the Low Countries. However, the reality of the Allied landings in France was to prevent the Soviet armies from steamrolling Western Europe every bit as it was to defeat Nazi Germany. However, Hitler had in his grasp the weapon to stop the Allied invasion in its tracks and never employed it.

In 1936, Dr. Gerhard Schrader, working on a new insecticide, invented nerve gas. Tabun, as it was called, was the first of the second generation of chemical weapons. Four years later, Schrader invented Sarin, which was more lethal than Tabun. Later in the war, the more virulent Soman was invented.

Nerve gas was many times more lethal than the first generation of chemical weapons employed in the First World War, like phosgene, chlorine, and mustard. The protective gear available to Allied troops in 1944 was for the first-generation agents and therefore worthless against nerve gas. Unlike the first-generation agents, which attacked the respiratory system like chlorine and phosgene or burned the skin like the blister gas mustard, Tabun attacked the nervous system. Messages from the brain are sent through the body's nervous system by the chemical cholinesterase. Messages are countermanded by the chemical acetylcholine. Nerve gas attacks acetylcholine, thereby inducing such fatal results as asphyxiation. By June 1944, Hitler had thousands of tons of

Tabun, enough to drench Allied troops when they landed. So the question remains, why didn't he use it?

Ardent Nazis like Joseph Goebbels, Robert Ley and Martin Bormann urged the Fuhrer to do so. Some theorize that, having been gassed himself in World War I, Hitler knew what it was like and therefore refrained from using it. This assumption is rather weak since Hitler took to gassing millions of so-called racial undesirables in the death camps. The more plausible theory is that of the objections raised by his chemical warfare advisor, Amos Ambros. Ambros intimated that many of the chemical compounds inherent in nerve gas had appeared in western chemical journals. This meant that the Allies had nerve gas, too. In actuality, the Allies were working on the revolutionary insecticide DDT. Such was the misconception of the Allied chemical warfare effort by the Nazis. Conversely, the Allies had no idea of the existence of nerve gas until the defeat of Nazi Germany!

Six decades after the demise of the Third Reich, misconceptions as to the collapse of the Soviet Union persist. Take the example of Pope John Paul II. This fascinating and significant individual will certainly leave an indelible mark not only on the history of the Church, but on history itself. This nomadic cleric traveled thousands of miles to many countries. He put a good face upon the Church with his globe-trotting and promotions of peace and love among nations. Having come from Poland, he had a firsthand knowledge of life under the heavy hand of authoritarian rule. He was recognized as a champion of people's rights. His effectiveness can certainly be discerned by the Soviet attempt to silence him with a Bulgarian gunman. Yet during the worldwide-televised funeral of the pontiff, much was made by the network analysts of his contribution to the collapse of the Soviet Empire. But just how much of an impact did he have?

Substantial, without question, but hardly decisive when measured against two other events of greater significance, the first being the election of Ronald Reagan to the presidency of the United States. Reagan's plan to humble the Soviet Union was simple as it was truly American: attack the problem with money, and lots of it. During the 1980s, the United States embarked on a weapons-building binge that the Soviet Union could not afford to match. It seemed the Republican administration had correctly assessed their adversary. The Soviet Union may have been a military superpower, but economically it was a Third-World power. In short, any nation that ranks sixty-third in the world in living standards has little hope of matching wallets with the United States.

The second factor was Afghanistan. For ten long, bloody years, the half-starved, ill-clothed, under-armed fighters there faced the Soviet occupiers in the barren mountain wastes. And they proved their mettle to the world. With eventual U.S. support of money and guns, they evicted the invader. But the cost did not come cheap. Estimates of the dead ranged from 500,000 to one million. But that victory was infectious. In Poland, East Germany, Hungary, Czechoslovakia, and the Baltic States, people rose up and forced not only a Soviet retreat, but the dissolution of Moscow's ill-gotten empire.

It seems, then, that the primary cause of the downfall of the Soviet Empire was due less to rhetoric as it was to the age-old formula of blood, money, and guns. While there is no substitute for peace, history, it seems, has been one long litany of conflict. History also shows that be they democratic or authoritarian, states desire to be autonomous. War provides the state with the alternative to achieve a strategic goal or defend its interests. This is why war will never be successfully outlawed. Rest assured for as long as man walks the earth, there will always be war. This is because war is man's oldest drama. The cast of characters may change, but the basic plot remains the same. Or does it? What about the ongoing plot in Iraq?

History will record the fact that on March 19, 2003, the armies of the United States and Britain invaded Iraq. Many a pretext has been voiced by the Bush administration to justify this course of action. Among their roster of reasons was that of bringing democracy to a population long denied their right to representative government. A noble cause, indeed, but one within the realm of reality?

When the Soviet Union collapsed, Russia supposedly embarked on the road to democracy. However, Victor Putin, former KGB functionary, a leader President George W. Bush once lavished with much praise, saw fit to restrict freedom of the press, freedom of speech, and freedom of assembly. If after nearly twenty years the success of democracy is in doubt with a people who have lived under authoritarian rule for a thousand years, how is democracy to take root and flourish with a people who have lived under authoritarian rule for many centuries before the birth of Christ?

For years America held the moral high ground with respects to human rights, freedom of expression, and representative government. And nowhere was it higher than immediately after September 11, 2001. But just as quickly was the high ground frittered away. Abu Ghraib, Guantanamo Bay, secret prisons, torture, unwarranted phone taps, and the aggrandizement of private property to satisfy the avarice of wealthy developers at the expense of the average American citizen. These are hardly the functions of a nation that claims to be the gold standard for the inalienable rights of man. The stench of repression cannot be covered up by the perfume of security. The need for security in the wake of the dastardly blow by al-Qaeda is beyond question. But for the sake of the rights and freedoms we enjoy and, at times, take for granted and which, in times past have been so painfully preserved, the American people should seek guidance in the words of one of its founding fathers. For, as Ben Franklin observed, "Those that can give up essential liberty to obtain a little temporary safety, deserve neither liberty or safety."

If the *National Geographic* poll of May 2006 is any guide, then there is cause for concern. A canvass was taken of young people between the ages of eighteen and twenty-four. It seems that following the devastating affects that Hurricane Katrina had wrought upon the Mississippi Delta area, one-third of those polled still could not find Louisiana on a map. Nearly half could not identify Mississippi. Equally distressing is the fact that at the time of this writing, after more than 3,900 Americans have been killed in Iraq, six of ten questioned could not find the war-torn country on a map. Seventy-five percent thought English was the most widely spoken native language. Apparently it had not occurred to any of these folks that more than twenty percent of the world's population is Chinese.

Geographic illiteracy translates into historical ignorance. This can be true anywhere you go. In fact, where I live in southern Connecticut, Fairfield County is considered one of the most affluent areas in the United States. Indeed, to put it bluntly, it is a county teeming with America's royalty. But even here, in an area oozing with cash, the almighty greenback cannot cure ignorance. Not long ago in the town in which I reside, two graduates of one of the local high schools told me that the atomic bombings of Hiroshima and Nagasaki occurred before the attack on Pearl Harbor. This pair is the product of a board of education that annually trumpets the success of its Black History Month program. While it is important to recall the struggle of the black man in the American saga, it is indeed apparent that other aspects of American history are not being given the proper attention.

On History: A Treatise does not pretend to offer itself as a panacea for the above. No book can do that, or can any writer or teacher. Its objective is to stimulate the reader to think. To think freely is a hallmark of the freedom of expression. *On History: A Treatise* was written with no other purpose in mind. If you agree with some of its assertions and conclusions, fine (hopefully not every one of them, for the unanimity of opinion can at times be as detrimental as ignorance). If you are not in agreement with its assessments, that is fine, too, for the unfettered exchange of ideas is a prerequisite to the survival of a free society.

CHAPTER 1

Legacy of the Little Red Schoolhouse

"Reason has never failed men. Only force and repression have made the wrecks of the world."
William Allen White

At 2:41 a.m., May 7, 1945, in a little red schoolhouse in Reims, France, five men affixed their signatures to a document of unconditional surrender: General Walter Bedell Smith of the United States; General Ivan Suslaparov of the Soviet Union; General Francois Savez of France; Admiral Hans von Friedeberg and General Alfred Jodl of Germany.

These five men validated more than just the Allied triumph over the Pact of Steel. They ratified the end of a conflict that began in 1914. A European conflict motivated by European issues, but which drew into its swirling vortex nations from around the globe. A conflict that, in the end, was decided not by Europeans, but by outsiders: the United States and the Soviet Union.

The French Revolution of 1789 opened a Pandora's Box of change that challenged monarchical rule in Europe. Political liberalism, nationalism, anti-colonialism, and the rise of the welfare state swept across the Continent during the nineteenth century, fueled by the exploding Industrial Revolution and the growing power of the middle class. By 1914, the royal houses of Europe—the Romanovs, Hohenzollerns, Hapsburgs, Ottomans, and the Hanovers—seemed oblivious to the fact that they were fast going the way of the dinosaur. They continued to play the noble pastime of chess on the map board of Europe: moving armies like pawns, engaging in dubious alliances, and chasing dangerous spheres of influence.

Yet the time bomb that had begun ticking in France in 1789 exploded in Sarajevo in 1914. The intermarriage of nobility proved ineffective as a prophylactic to the civil war that consumed it. A war that devoured an entire generation. A war that saw the rise of the first Marxist-Leninist state and the collapse of the Russian, German, Ottoman, and Austro-Hungarian empires.

The discords that gave impulse to the War to End All Wars remained unresolved at Versailles. The Great Powers redrew the Continental map with little regard for ethnic concerns or nationalist passions. Britain and France clung greedily to their colonial empires. Italy, which earned little in the way of spoils despite changing to the winning side, endorsed Mussolini's promise to recapture the glory that was once Rome's.

In the Pacific, too, Japan profited from Germany's misfortune and Allied preoccupation with Europe to expand its empire, threatening American, British, French, and Dutch interests.

But it was in Germany where the continuation of the European civil war and the ensuing drift toward global conflagration occurred.

The Allies forced Germany to accept full responsibility for the Great War and the reparations that followed. French and Belgian troops occupied the Ruhr. The once-vaunted German armed forces were reduced to a paltry 100,000 men and denied airplanes and submarines.

But the Allies failed to dissolve the German General Staff. More than simply a military high command, the General Staff fomented the myth that the Fatherland had been stabbed in the back by democrats, socialists, and Jews. Left virtually unchecked, the General Staff worked tirelessly to undermine German democracy and foster rearmament. Though in the end, this powerful clique of Prussian aristocrats was made to swear unconditional obedience to a vulgar little corporal named Adolf Hitler.

Though not of noble birth, the heir to the Kaiser was a product of the Austro-Hungarian Empire. A comical-looking Austrian with a Charlie Chaplin mustache who, with his guttural gift of gab, stoked the fires of nationalist fervor and bent the German millions to his indomitable will. With deft political skill, he shanghaied the obedience of the armed forces and dealt with his rivals with unabashed ruthlessness.

Beginning with the Rhineland in 1936, Hitler faced world leaders at the brink and won bloodless victory after bloodless victory. The League of Nations proved powerless to stop him. Britain and France, bled white in the trenches, had no stomach for further conflict. The United States enjoyed the last years of isolation, comfortably ensconced in the false sense of security provided by two oceans, while Bolshevist Russia was ostracized by the world community—except by the one nation which would later stab it in the back, Nazi Germany.

With his thirst for conquest whetted, Hitler invaded Poland and plunged the Continent into war. The nations of Western Europe fell like ninepins to his panzers. By June 1941, he had avenged the hated Versailles Treaty and had won the European civil war. Uniting the Continent under the crooked cross of Fascism, Adolf Hitler had accomplished by forces of arms what the framers of Maastricht later planned on paper.

Drang nach Osten was the age-old German desire to expand to the East. In *Mein Kampf,* the National Socialist bible, Hitler outlined a plan known as *Lebensraum,* by which the Germans would carve out living space in the East at the expense of the "subhuman" Slavs already living there.

On June 22, 1941, Hitler fulfilled medieval German ambitions by hurling 139 divisions at the Soviet Union. On December 7, the Japanese bombed Pearl Harbor. Three days later, Hitler declared war on the United States. Thus the conflict became a struggle for global domination, a struggle the Third Reich proved unable to win.

Hitler lost his bid for master of the world on five fronts. First, he lost the intelligence war. Allied decryption of Axis ciphers proved decisive in shortening the war and saving lives. Second, he lost the battle of the Atlantic, thereby guaranteeing the Allies an uninterrupted flow of supplies from the Arsenal of Democracy. Third, he failed to conquer England. The Allies turned the island kingdom into an unsinkable aircraft carrier from which their bombers pummeled the Reich and later into a springboard for the invasion of France. Fourth, from June 22, 1941, to May 7, 1945, most of the Wehrmacht was mired in the endless steppes of the East and consumed there in the greatest land war yet waged. The campaign in Russia decided who was going to win the land war in World War II. And lastly, German production of war materiel was far outstripped by that of the Allies.

―――

From V-E Day to the collapse of the Soviet Union, Europeans did not control their own destiny. It was American and Soviet military power that ensured the peace of Europe, extinguished the flames of extreme nationalism, and helped bring an end to European imperialism. Germany, the key to peace in central Europe, was occupied by the victorious Allies. The German General Staff was dissolved. The power of the aristocracy was broken. And German democracy was allowed to take root and flourish.

Today in the post-Cold War era, Europeans are attempting to forge their own destiny for the first time in over half a century. France and Germany appear to have buried the hatchet (for the time being) and seem intent on leading an uncertain European Union. Their voices were the Continent's loudest in opposition to the American desire to topple Saddam Hussein. French, German, and Russian leadership saw cooperation with the UN as the proper course for reining in Saddam and to allow inspectors more time to locate alleged weapons of mass destruction. The reality was that France and Russia were heavily invested in Iraq's oil industry. Both were owed many billions by Saddam's regime. Germany threw in its lot with France and Russia, needing to absolve itself of its Hitlerian stigma and exercise its political muscle in the post-Soviet era. The fact that Germany played a role in building up Iraq's chemical warfare capability was conveniently forgotten.

Not to be left out in the political cold, Britain cast its lot with the United States. The idea being that Britain's military muscle could maintain London's political clout in the post-Cold War, much like it did in the Persian Gulf conflict of 1991. London realizes that the United States is still the major arbiter of peace. And by attaching itself to that reality, it still would be able to perform its age-old function of swing power in response to Franco-German hegemony in Continental politics.

For the present, the United States finds itself the world's sole superpower. The urge to act unilaterally instead of multilaterally is proving difficult to resist. French and German concerns here are justified, especially in light of American initiatives in Iraq after 9/11. For despite its limitations, the UN is still a viable forum for airing grievances and must not be allowed to go the way of the League of Nations. But in the present state of the world, UN-sponsored initiatives will be difficult to enact and enforce. The world is no longer divided into two spheres of influence, and, therefore, is in much greater danger of conflict. So just what is the legacy of the little red schoolhouse? It is six decades after the greatest war in man's history claimed more than 50,000,000 lives. Yet after such profligacy in human life, man is no nearer to peace than when he first took up the cudgel against his fellow man. He still engages in dangerous spheres of influence, slavery, genocide, terrorism, and repressions too numerous to mention. Indeed it is clear that with history as a guide, the outlook for peace in the years ahead is doubtful at best.

Chapter 2

Swing Power

"History repeats itself, and that's one of the things wrong with history." Clarence Darrow

ON HISTORY

How many times have we heard the phrase "Those who cannot remember the past are doomed to repeat it"? Too many, perhaps? Enough to where we have become immune to its meaning, in much the same way as our olfactory nerves become desensitized to an odor from prolonged exposure? Possibly. It might help to explain the world's passivity to genocide in Cambodia when the memories of the Holocaust were still so hauntingly fresh. Or consider the rocketing of the *USS Stark* in the Persian Gulf in 1987. Did Washington fail to see in this attack the prospect of much greater Iraqi bellicosity? Apparently nothing was learned from Japan's sinking of the *Panay* in 1937.

Today we find that not all the lessons resulting from the attack on Pearl Harbor have been forgotten—on both sides of the Pacific. For instance, during the standoff with the Soviet Union, an ever-vigilant intelligence community kept America's shores safe from surprise attack. In Japan, it was realized that the Hondas and Toyotas that jammed the holds of her container ships today have accomplished much, much more than the Mitsubishis and Nakajimas that crammed the decks of her aircraft carriers yesterday. This development has been seen by some Americans as an economic Pearl Harbor. This is a rather simplistic view that fails to recognize that most of the economic ills that plague the United States are largely domestic in manufacture and not the aftermath of another surprise attack by the "Yellow Peril."

To be sure, though, the Japanese must bear some of the blame for the growing rift that resulted during the 1980s and 90s. They had failed to open many of their markets to foreigners, a form of protectionism that had its roots based in the medieval Japanese distrust of outside influence. Before World War II, this phenomenon was exploited by the militarists bent on organizing Japan for conquest. Following the war, it was exploited by her leading industrialists seeking to assure their profits.

By the 1990s, the United States and Japan accounted for some thirty-three percent of the global economic output. If the New World Order as envisioned by President George H.W. Bush was to have any chance for success, then U.S.-Japanese cooperation was essential. That cooperation had to be based on a clear understanding of national interests and respect for cultural sovereignty, seek to stimulate competition but frustrate confrontation, and act as a model of interdependency and global trade to which the world could aspire. *The miscalculations of the 1920s and 30s that led to the bloodletting of the 1940s must not be repeated!*

But there are other lessons, too. Lessons in history which need to be heeded if world peace and stability are to endure. We will now take a look at some of those lessons and analyze them and note their importance at the time of the Persian Gulf War, as the United States sought to redefine its role as the world's foremost global power in the post-Cold War.

In 1992, the United States found itself in a world not too unlike that of 1918. The demise of the Soviet Union, like the collapse of Imperial Germany and the Austro-Hungarian Empire, eliminated a bond that held many nations together in a common purpose and called into question old alliances and partnerships. In Eastern Europe, pent-up forces of liberalism and nationalism had once again turned the area into a cauldron of political and ethnic turmoil. In the former Soviet Union, dissident republics sought out their own identities in an uncertain commonwealth. In Western Europe, France and Germany took the lead in forging a United States of Europe, in an attempt by the Continental powers to reassert control over their own affairs for the first time since 1945. While in the Pacific, the United States and Japan tried to come to grips with their competing interests now that the common enemy had been defeated.

But just as in 1918, a growing number of Americans saw an opportunity to concentrate on domestic problems at the expense of global commitments and for reasons comparable to those of seven decades before. For instance, in February 1919, some three million people were out of work, at that time about ten percent of the workforce, as the nation struggled through the conversion from a war time to a peacetime economy. In 1991, the United States was in a recession, which saw more than seven percent of the workforce jobless, with at least one out of every five without a job at one time or another. As with Woodrow Wilson, who had been busy at Versailles with the peace treaty, President Bush had been accused of paying too much attention to foreign affairs at the expense of domestic policy.

In November that same year, voters in Pennsylvania took matters into their own hands. They elected to the Senate Democratic challenger Harris Wofford, a protectionist who believed in handling Japan with anything but kid gloves, over well-known Republican Dick Thornburg. In the Republican Party, too, conservative Pat Buchanan tossed his hat into the ring of presidential politics, running a platform based on attacking the out-of-balanced federal budget and promising help to the home front instead of devoting America's treasury to some uncertain new world order. And in an example of extremist politics, David Duke, former Grand Wizard of the Ku Klux Klan, made an unsuccessful bid for the governorship of Louisiana. Following that, he, too, threw in his hat for the Republican presidential nomination.

President Bush, it seemed, got the message. He delayed assistance to the former Soviet Union, his planned trip to Asia, and work on the free trade agreement with Mexico.

Though more Americans still favored a global role, the rising tide of isolationism could no longer be ignored.

But while it is the essence of the American political system that all quarters of the electorate—regardless of race, creed, gender, or persuasion—have the right to participation, it is just as important to be mindful of the danger of tilting too far to the left or to the right. How ironic it must have seemed to the world then that the leader of the most powerful nation, the acknowledged champion of freedom and human rights, a nation that was at the heart and soul of resistance to such tyrannies as Nazi Germany and the Soviet Union, should now decide to play appeasement politics at home with a movement that, historically at any rate, had little regard for political and economic liberalism.

Originally the Isolationist-Conservative camp was a collusion of big business and government that, following World War I, decided to put the nation back on its prewar course of "normalcy." What this actually meant was a resumption of the pursuit of the Almighty Dollar by the privileged, who were eager to exploit their new wealth generated from the war. In this they tolerated no intrusions whether internal or external. This meant continued enforcement of the wartime Sedition Act (a piece of legislation of the most dubious constitutionality) to deal with "anti-Americanism" in word or print; suppressing the labor movement and condemning unionism as a form of Bolshevism; continued discrimination and restricting the immigration of selected races, in particular, the Japanese; and ensuring the profits of American business by limiting competition from abroad with protectionist measures, a similar sentiment echoed by

American businessmen in the early 1990s in response to Japanese competition.

If President Bush forgot his history, movements such as the modern-day feminists did not. They saw the new Isolationist-Conservative camp as a threat to civil rights. And they had no intention of giving up gains made on such issues as abortion, equal opportunity, and sexual harassment. Such was their opposition to the Clarence Thomas nomination to the Supreme Court. As to the Capitol Hill hearings and public debate on whether he had actually harassed Anita Hill was irrelevant when compared to the underlying essence of the case, that being those from the left did not want another candidate from the right on the nation's highest court.

Yet the real tragedy of isolationist thinking is the failure to grasp America's standing as a global power. George Washington's warning against foreign entanglements was one of the principles of the original America Firsters. Yet their literal interpretation of its meanings was as unimaginative as it was dangerous. After all, did not the fledgling colonies ally themselves with France to throw off the British yoke? Later did not the young nation open embassies abroad? Was not the Monroe Doctrine a foreign policy initiative that bound America to its neighbors to the north and to the south? It stands to reason then that if the world was being traversed by wood and sail in 1797, inventions such as the airplane rendered isolationism virtually obsolete by 1920.

By then the United States was truly a global power. Its growing economic interdependency rendered the traditional barriers of the Atlantic and Pacific totally breachable. But the Maginot mentality of the isolationists persisted, barring participation in the League of Nations at a time when American support was crucial to a Britain and France bled white in the trenches. This together with western ostracizing of the Soviet Union helped to spur the rise of Fascism, Nazism, and Japanese militarism. Soon aggression was feeding on itself, and the League's demise was all but a foregone conclusion. And with it went the dream that the Great War was to be the last war.

The Firsters of 1990 were just as myopic. They failed to see past protectionism and buy American slogans to realize that economic interdependency was more important than ever before. For example, 1989 to 1992 U.S. businesses saw their domestic profits fall by more than twenty percent while their foreign profits rose by some fifteen percent. Similarly in a five-year period that ended in 1990, U.S. imports rose by some $130 billion; while during the same period, which ended in 1990, U.S. exports rose by some $167 billion, which was forty percent of the growth of GNP. Approximately 20,000 jobs were being generated for every $1 billion in exports.

But nowhere was the prospect of repeating the mistakes of the 1920s and 30s greater than in Europe, particularly Eastern Europe. For most of the twentieth century, this area, including the Balkans, had been a *Cordon Sanitaire.* In 1919, France saw it as a way to hem in a resurgent Germany and act as a barrier against the westward spread of Bolshevism. In 1941, Germany used it as a springboard for its invasion of the Soviet Union. In 1945, the Soviet Union used it as a buffer zone against its former Western Allies.

With the collapse of the Eastern Bloc, this area became a vacuum. The only nation with the political and economic strength to fill the void was Germany. Paris joined with Bonn to create a "United States of Europe" primarily to check German hegemony. Britain, concerned not only about what a European confederation would do to its sovereignty, was also concerned about the effect an exclusive European foreign and defense policy would have on NATO. For Britain traditionally has been Europe's swing power. The nation that saw to it that no other power dominated the continent, a role which, in view of her current political and economic status, she was no longer able to perform—without U.S. support.

British concerns were justified. A continued American presence in Europe was required. With the collapse of the Soviet Union and victory in the Gulf War, the United States was the only nation with the political, military, and economic power to lead a coalition against any power that felt confident enough to assert itself in a belligerent manner. The immediate threat was the new Commonwealth of Independent States, where an economic crisis made for dire political uncertainties. Anarchy and civil war were very real possibilities, making it a breeding ground for Fascism or Islamic Fundamentalism. And with nuclear weapons in the picture, America's strategic arsenal provided a needed counterbalance. Yet, as the Gulf War showed, there were limits to American power.

The Persian Gulf War was the first real test of the so-called

New World Order. In an impressive demonstration of collective security, nations put aside their differences to meet the common enemy. The result was that the aggressor was decisively defeated in a swift and crushing military campaign; the sovereignty of a tiny member of the international community was restored; and international peace and stability were preserved.

Yet the reality of the war was quite different. It was not fought so much to liberate Kuwait as it was to protect Saudi Arabia from Saddam's hordes. Oil was the reason for war—on both sides of the line. For Saddam, it meant increasing his share of OPEC reserves so as to be better able to set the price of crude, thereby financing Iraq's $100 billion debt from its war with Iran on the backs of the cartel's customers. For industrialized nations such as the United States, already in the throes of a worldwide recession, paying such tribute was an anathema.

Fortunately for the United States, Saddam's timing was as poor as his understanding of recent history. He failed to see that the Cold War was winding down and that the Soviet Union would be in no position to help. He judged U.S. resolve on such issues as the Iranian hostage crisis, the U.S. retreat from Beirut after the bombing of the Marines' barracks and the rocketing of the *USS Stark* by an Iraqi jet in 1987. He believed, too, that the Vietnam syndrome still applied. But he also failed to see that twice during the 1980s, when its economic interests were threatened, the United States acted with force.

In Grenada, President Reagan sent in U.S. forces to rescue American students caught in the middle of a violent coup. At the same time, the international airport on the island was neutralized. This airport was dangerously close to the shipping lanes. From it Soviet and Cuban pilots would have been able to fly out into the South Atlantic to interdict tanker traffic from the Middle East to the United States in time of crisis. In Panama, allegedly in support of the popularly elected government, President Bush sent in troops to arrest former strongman Manuel Noriega for his part in smuggling drugs to the United States. But the president's overriding concern of course was the security of the Panama Canal.

The coalition forged by President Bush and James Baker for action in the Persian Gulf was a *tour de force* in diplomacy. Their use of the UN as a way around Congress to secure the military option could serve as a blueprint for future administrations. But the decision to use the world body was based on considerations other than that of simple politics. After all, the United States was not the only nation benefiting from Middle East oil, so why should it be expected to bear the entire burden of defending it? Yet the question of assistance was one of need and not fairness, because the United States could not afford to go to war.

That the budget deficit was sapping America's strength was apparent. The economic foundation that had once buttressed the great Arsenal of Democracy had developed chips and cracks. What had once accounted for some forty percent of global economic output had been reduced to 23 percent. An ever-increasing budget deficit had grown to such proportions that it was costing U.S. taxpayers $.20 out of every dollar he or she paid in federal taxes just to service the interest on the swelling debt. This meant that to service the budget proper, Washington was working on just $.80 on the dollar. In consequence, the ability to pursue foreign policy objectives unilaterally had diminished. This was the president's dilemma in prosecuting the war. The need to act multilaterally mortgaged his freedom of action to the political considerations of his coalition partners, especially to those of his Arab allies. Their concern was that a prostrate Iraq would no longer prove a bulwark against fundamentalist Iran. Therefore a brilliant military campaign was cut short, allowing the bulk of Iraq's Republican Guards to escape. Preservation of the Guards doomed any hopes the Bush administration might have had of the Kurds and Shias staging a successful uprising. It is ironic to note that President Bush himself, who once likened Saddam Hussein to Adolf Hitler, made the same decision the Fuhrer made at Dunkirk in 1940, in allowing enemy forces to slip away.

Yet conservative Arab leaders feared the promise of political liberalism and respect for human rights offered by the New World Order every bit as much as they did the mullahs in Tehran. The decline of the Soviet Union served to remind them of how fragile the hold on power can be. Hence Hussein's ruthless repressions at home following the war served to ensure that the fever of dissent would not cross his borders.

Washington's complicity in maintaining the status quo in the Middle East compromised the first real test of the New World Order. Quite simply, economic realities took precedence over wishful idealism. Oil was the lifeblood of the economy, and any clots would endanger survival, let alone a lasting economic recovery. And to make certain there were no more clots, a permanent military presence was established. It was merely a transfer of the Cold War strategy to the Middle East. As long as dependence on foreign oil exists, the American people will have to get used to the idea of playing powerbroker in an area of extreme political uncertainty. This includes the employment of the military option when necessary to make sure that no one player dominates the field. Washington merely reprised the role Britain played in Europe for over four hundred years.

Chapter 3

Killers In White Coats

"I swear by Apollo the physician, by Aesculapius, Hygeia and Panacea, and I take witness all the gods, all the goddesses, to keep according to my ability and my judgment the following oath:

> "To consider dear to me as my parents him who taught me this art; to live in common with him and if necessary to share my goods with him; to look upon his children as my own brothers, to teach them this art if they so desire without fee or written promise; to impart to my sons and the sons of the master who taught me and the disciples who have enrolled themselves and have agreed to the rules of the profession, but to these alone, the precepts and the instruction. I will prescribe regimen for the good of my patients according to my ability and my judgment and never do harm to anyone. To please no one will I prescribe a deadly drug, or give advice which may cause his

death. Nor will I give a woman a pessary to procure abortion. But I will preserve the purity of my life and my art. I will not cut for stone, even for patients in whom the disease is manifest; I will leave this operation to be performed by practitioners (specialists in this art). In every house where I come I will enter only for the good of my patients, keeping myself far from all intentional ill-doing and all seduction, especially from the pleasures of love with women or with men, be they free or slaves. All that may come to my knowledge in the exercise of my profession or in daily commerce with men, which ought not to be spread abroad, I will keep secret and never reveal. If I keep this oath faithfully, may I enjoy my life and practice my art, respected by all men and in all times; but if I swerve from it or violate it, may the reverse be my lot." The Hippocratic Oath

---

Late in 1938, the father of a deformed child, a man by the name of Knauer, petitioned the Reich Chancellery in Berlin. The communication aroused the interest of Adolf Hitler, who sent his personal physician and intimate, Dr. Karl Brandt, to the University of Leipzig to investigate.

Dr. Brandt found the child exactly as the father had described—deaf, blind, and missing a leg and part of an arm. He ordered the immediate *Gnadentod* (mercy death) of the child. He assured the doctors that any legal action taken against them would be suppressed by the Fuhrer.

The destruction of the Knauer child was the test case for organized medical killing in Nazi Germany and marked the end of sterilization as the principal means of dealing with mental defectives and the incurably physically handicapped. By the following spring, doctors, nurses, and midwives were filling out questionnaires for every newborn. The forms were then sent for evaluation to the Reich Committee for the Scientific Registration of Serious Hereditary and Congenital Diseases.

Once a child had been diagnosed as incurable, he or she was sent to one of thirty centers known as Reich Committee Institutions for Treatment. Parents were told that the transfer was due to a change in the child's condition and that alternative therapy or surgery was necessary.

The alternative therapy was death, usually by injections of morphine-scopolamine or luminal ground up in the child's food. Records were falsified and the parents were notified of the child's unfortunate demise.

By summer, the age limit of three had been raised to sixteen and the grounds for eligibility had been liberalized. No longer were children being terminated simply because of idiocy or missing limbs; but for diagnoses ranging from mongolism to borderline juvenile delinquency to those afflicted with "inferior genes," a National Socialist euphemism for Jews, gypsies, and others considered non-German.

By July 1939, with the killing of racially valueless children well underway, Hitler prepared to rid Germany of the infirm and insane among the adult population. T4, as the program came to be known, not only became broader in scope than the children's program, but became an all-out effort by the Hitlerites to purge useless eaters from the Third Reich. In this the German medical community became a willing partner, as there was never a shortage of doctors or nurses to carry out the Nazis' murderous scheme. Indeed many of the medical personnel came from the ranks of the SS, as Heinrich Himmler came to view racial hygiene as another way to Aryanize the German race.

Yet it was the institutionalization of medical killing that made T4 so murderously effective. An intricate network of medicine, government, and transportation was woven and honed to such a deadly degree of efficiency, until organized medical killing became systematic genocide.

In July 1939, Hitler conferred with Hans Lammers, head of the Reich Chancellery, and SS-Obergruppenfuhrer Dr. Leonardo Conti. Dr. Conti was head of the health department in the Ministry of Interior and, as such, was selected to head the program to eliminate the adult incurables. But when Dr. Conti requested a written authorization, Hitler replaced him with Dr. Victor Brandt, while Lammers was replaced with Reich Leader Philip Bouhler.

Bouhler and Brandt were prototypical Hitler loyalists, trusted party hacks that could be depended upon to eschew the demands for legality and fiscal accountability to which the ordinary government bureaucrat was subject. For Hitler was well aware of the unpopularity of physician-assisted suicide in Germany and had no wish to chance a public disclosure of his plans to annihilate a helpless segment of the population.

Nevertheless, in early October, the need to formalize the program forced the Fuhrer to issue just such an authorization. The decree, written by Hitler on his personal stationery and backdated to September 1, read as follows:

Reich Leader Bouhler and Dr. Brandt are charged with the responsibility for expanding the authority of physicians, to be designated by name, to the end that patients considered incurable according to the best available human judgment of their state of health, can be granted a mercy death.

By issuing the decree on his personal stationery, Hitler made his decision appear as a private matter and not a decision as a head of state; while the September 1 date of issue coincided with the opening of the Polish campaign, which Hitler thought would make the decree more palatable to the German people if it were made to appear as a war measure.

At the outset, the program was run out of Philip Bouhler's office in the Reich Chancellery. The Reich Leader's address was Tiergartenstrasse 4, which gave rise to the program's infamous name, T4.

Bouhler chose Dr. Victor Brack to run the day-to-day operations of T4, which was known throughout the Reich Chancellery as Department II. The cover organization was given the benign nomenclature Reich Work Group of Sanatoriums and Nursing Homes.

Like the children's program, selection for death was based on information obtained from the questionnaires that doctors and nurses filled out for each and every patient. The forms contained the usual biographical and symptomatic information, so that unsuspecting physicians and patients were inculcated with the fiction of normal administrative and scientific functions.

But one section was specific in its interrogation and

required a check in the appropriate space to determine the sufferer's exemption from work. There were four categories from which to choose: The first listing such debilitations as schizophrenia, epilepsy, senility, retardation, encephalitis, and therapy-resistant paralysis. Second, criminal insanity. Third, a five-year history of institutionalization. And fourth, a lack of German citizenship or lack of German blood—that is, Jews, gypsies, Negroes, etc.

Each questionnaire was reviewed by a panel of three medical experts, usually psychiatrists. Upon completion of his review, each panelist would mark the space provided on the lower left corner with a "+" in red pencil for death, a "–" in blue pencil for life, and a "?" for further review. The questionnaires were then forwarded to a senior expert who was not bound by the findings of the previous reviewers. Once he rendered a decision and affixed his signature, the candidate's fate was decided.

But the reviews were cursory at best, as each reviewer poured over no less than one hundred cases at a time. And as the program expanded, so did the workload. For instance, Dr. Hermann Pfannmuller reviewed 2,109 cases in one seventeen-day period. Little wonder then that such heavy workloads and slipshod reviews cost thousands their lives.

Death lists were drawn up and forwarded to the Common Welfare Ambulance Service. Pick-up schedules were arranged so that patients could be made ready to travel with their belongings, valuables, and case histories. The buses of the Common Welfare Ambulance Service were manned by SS personnel clad in white coats or uniforms of doctors, nurses, and medical attendants. The windows of the buses were blackened or shielded to keep patients from public view. Documentation furnished allowed the drivers to pass unchallenged through any checkpoint.

Patients were taken to one of the "transit" or "observation" centers, usually a state hospital located near one of the killing centers. Letters sent to the families concerned explained the transfer as a war-related measure. Follow-up letters reassured families of their loved ones' safe arrival, adding that the demands of the war on the Reich's medical personnel made visits out of the question and that further communication was dependent upon a change in the patient's condition. A change in condition nearly always referred to the patient's death.

From the transit centers, patients were taken to one of the six killing centers located at Bernburg, Brandenburg, Grafeneck, Hadamar, Hartheim, and Sonnenstein. All were converted hospitals or nursing homes, except Brandenburg, which had been a prison. All were surrounded by high walls, so that disturbances went unnoticed by the outside world.

Patients were killed within twenty-four hours of arrival at a killing center. The standard method of execution was lethal injection, consisting usually of a combination of morphine, scopolamine, curare, and prussic acid.

As T4 was broadened to deal with a wider variety of useless eaters, the syringe proved less than adequate as a method of extermination. There were just too many patients, and they took too long to die. What was needed was a more efficient method of killing and disposal, one which would not only keep pace with the growing number of patients, but kill them without a trace.

In the spring of 1940, Christian Wirth, of the SS *Kripo,* or criminal police, working in conjunction with the T4 staff at Brandenburg, supervised the construction of the first gas chamber, a room fitted with sealed doors and windows, wooden benches, and bogus showerheads. On hand for the initial demonstration was a select group of officials, including Dr. Brandt and Dr. Brack. The objects of the exercise were four mentally retarded men.

Outside the chamber, two SS chemists started a motor, which pumped in carbon monoxide. In ten minutes, the four men inside were dead. The ventilation system cleared the chamber of gas in five minutes. Then a team of SS moved in. They loaded the corpses onto stretchers. The stretchers, which operated mechanically, lowered the bodies to the crematory below and then loaded them into the ovens to be burned.

The demonstration impressed both Dr. Brandt and Dr. Brack. And it was not long before the other killing centers were armed with gas chambers. Now each center had the capacity to kill twenty or thirty patients at a time versus the paltry five or six by injection.

Yet as the buses raced to keep the ovens stoked, another problem loomed for the Nazis, a problem that could not be buried under the mounting ashes of the dead. That problem was secrecy. From the occasional loose lips of a staffer to the sweet sickly smell belching from the chimneys, the veil of secrecy that enveloped T4 was beginning to unravel.

Children playing in the streets were beginning to recognize the speeding buses. In Hadamar they would say, "There goes the murder box again," or, "If you don't watch out, you'll be sent to bake in Hadamar."

More and more, people were beginning to question the bogus letters of condolences, demanding to know more about the whereabouts of their loved ones.

And then there were the church protests. Protestant Bishop Theophil Wurm of Wurttemberg wrote letters of protest to Reich Minister Wilhelm Frick and Franz Gurtner at the Reich Ministry of Justice. Pastor Paul Gerhard Braune and Pastor Friedrich von Bodelschwingh, director of the Bethel Hospital, wrote or spoke to many influential Nazis. One of Braune's letters even found its way to the Fuhrer himself, while Cardinal Michael Faulhaber of Munich caused a stir when one of his letters appeared in Sweden.

Catholic Cardinal Adolf Bertram and Bishop Heinrich Wienken, of the Fulda Conference of Bishops, wrote letters of protest and, in the case of Bishop Wienken, discussed ways of ceasing the killing with none other than Dr. Brack himself, but to no avail.

But the most powerful voice of dissent was that of Clemens Count von Galen, Bishop of Munster, and bearer of a name renowned throughout Germany for centuries. The homilies of this indomitable cleric in support of innocent life reverberated all the way to Berlin. But it was the sermon on August 5, 1941, that shook the very foundation of the Reich Chancellery itself. A shock multiplied a thousand-fold by leaflets of the reprinted sermon dropped from bombers of the RAF.

Many leading Nazis like Heinrich Himmler and Martin

Bormann wanted Bishop Galen executed. Hitler, both terrified and stung to fury, took counsel from Joseph Goebbels. The wily propaganda minister urged restraint in the face of creating an anti-Nazi martyr, since Catholic support was necessary for the struggle against Communist Russia. The Bishop's comeuppance could wait until after the war.

On August 24, 1941, Hitler ordered Dr. Brandt to cease the operations of T4.

Upwards of 100,000 people died under the auspices of T4, but the killing did not end with the termination of the program. Rather, the responsibility for racial hygiene passed from the hands of the German medical community to those of the SS.

The scope of racial hygiene as envisioned by Himmler and Heydrich was too much for the parochial confines of T4. Their diagnosis was simplistic as it was collective: All those with inferior genes were subject to the racial cure. The entire Reich was to be cleansed of Jews, gypsies, Slavs, and other so-called *untermensch* in a monumental effort that saw syringes and buses give way to gas chambers and trains.

Yet to fully comprehend the monstrosity of the deed, it is important to recognize T4 for what it really was. It was not euthanasia, though routinely it has been labeled as such. "Euthanasia," according to *Webster's,* is the practice of putting hopelessly sick persons or animals to death for reasons of mercy. T4 was not enacted for reasons of mercy. One would be hard pressed to find the word "mercy" in Nazi jargon. Rather, T4 was an attempt to use the medical community to purify the race of mental incompetents, the infirm, the aged, and all those other useless eaters deemed pollutants to racial purity.

T4, then, was organized medical killing. Where doctors, bureaucrats, and party hacks took it upon themselves to determine who lived or died. A National Socialist HMO with racial purity as its objective.

Could it happen again? Even here in the United States? Anything is possible. For after all the horrors of the Nazi program of genocide, extermination again reared its ugly head in such places as Cambodia, Rwanda, and the Balkans. So it is not inconceivable to consider the idea of organized medical killing in an era of abortion, gene-splicing, and stem-cell research. For in the industrialized world, people are living longer, a prospect that could clash with spiraling medical costs and public pressure to trim budgets. And in the era of the throwaway society, the infirm, the aged, and mental incompetents could very well be considered disposable. For the United States, baby-boomers are set to retire, which will put monstrous pressure on Social Security and the American medical community. Does this mean that those considered "incurable" will be deemed unnecessary in the preservation of fiscal solvency? The human population has grown by leaps and bounds in the modern era. So has man's capacity to kill. And it seems human life is no different, in the end, than any other commodity. The more of anything there is, the less value it has. The same seems to hold true for human life. Whether man is willing to admit it or not, such is the case. And this disregard for the sanctity of life bodes ill for the generations to come.

Chapter 4

Genzai Bakudan

"The essence of war is violence. Moderation in war is imbecility." Sir John "Jacky" Fisher

Ahead there was only destruction, total destruction. A wasteland of shattered buildings, incinerated homes, and scorched earth. A desolate moonscape that became more horrifying as the great steel prow cut lazily through the black waters, pushing through a flotsam of burned and bloated bodies that bobbed like corks in the creamy wake. Occupation troops were set to go ashore. They would face no opposition. Because, you see, the city was dead.

Sound like an ominous prophecy of Nostradamus? Or perhaps the opening scene of an episode from Rod Serling's *Twilight Zone*? No. It is the aftermath of Genzai Bakudan, the atomic bomb. It is Nagasaki as seen by my father from the bridge of the USS *Ottawa,* an attack transport loaded with marines. Weeks before, the B-29 *Bock's Car* dropped its deadly load, ending the war and proving Brigadier General Thomas Farrell correct. After witnessing the first explosion at Alamogordo, New Mexico, on July 16, 1945, the deputy commander of the Manhattan Project accurately observed, "The war's over. One or two of these things, and Japan will be finished." President Truman agreed. On August 2, he authorized the bomb's use.

The luckless city chosen to usher in the Atomic Age was Hiroshima. Hiroshima was home to an army transport base and food, ordnance, and clothing depots. There was also a large railway yard, electrical works, textile mills, oil-storage facilities, and a shipbuilding yard.

Commander of the 509th Composite Group, Colonel Paul Tibbets, would fly the bomb plane. His crew was as follows: Captain Robert A. Lewis, co-pilot; Major Thomas Ferebee, bombardier; Captain Theodore Van Kirk, navigator; Lieutenant Jacob Beser, radar countermeasures officer; Master Sergeant Wyatt A. Dusenbury, flight engineer; Staff Sergeant Joseph S. Stiborik, radar operator; Sergeant George R. Caron, tail gunner; Sergeant Robert A, Schumard, waist gunner; Pfc. Richard H. Nelson, radio operator. Also aboard was Navy Captain William S. "Deke" Parsons, who was in charge of the bomb, and his assistant Lieutenant Morris R. Jeppson.

Group insignias on the three planes making the flight

were removed; but Tibbets had his mother's name, *Enola Gay*, painted on the fuselage of his bomber.

The camera plane was to be piloted by Captain George R. Marquardt. While the B-29 armed with the instruments to measure the blast was to be piloted by Major Charles W. Sweeney. (Major Sweeney would later fly *Bock's Car* to Nagasaki, and become the only pilot to fly both atomic bomb missions.)

At Alamogordo, a plutonium bomb had been expended. But for Hiroshima, the *Enola Gay* would drop a uranium bomb. "Little Boy," as the bomb was called, was hoisted into the forward bomb bay the night before.

At 0245, August 6, 1945, *Enola Gay* lifted heavily off the crushed coral runway on Tinian. Marquardt and Sweeney followed at two-minute intervals.

Over the Pacific, Parsons and Jeppson armed the bomb.

Over Iwo Jima, Tibbets began the slow climb to attack altitude. The final decision to bomb the primary or alternate target, Kokura, rested on information collected by the weather planes flying ahead.

When they reached the Japanese coast, Tibbets' headphones began to crackle, "2/10 lower and middle lower, and 2/10 at 15,000 feet." Visual conditions over the primary target are excellent! Tibbets turned *Enola Gay* toward Hiroshima.

Tibbets began the bomb run from twenty-five miles out. At twelve miles, he said into his intercom, "It's yours."

Major Ferebee took control of the bomber. He lowered his left eye onto the Nordon bombsight and focused in.

Below, the Ota River snaked its way to a delta, where the tributaries splayed like seven spreading fingers.

Then the Aioi Bridge rolled into the crosshairs. "I got it!" announced the bombardier.

At fifteen minutes and seventeen seconds past eight, the bomb bay doors swung open. Ferebee watched Little Boy tumble out stern first, then nose over toward its target. "Bomb's away!"

Less 10,000 pounds, the lumbering Superfort shot up like a cork. Tibbets threw her into a simultaneous sixty-degree dive and 158-degree turn at a speed of 328 miles per hour.

Some 31,600 feet below the twisting bomber, 245,000 unsuspecting souls were going about their business.

Forty-three seconds later, a sky-searing flash, like the popping of a gigantic flashbulb, lit the morning sky and whited out the inside of the fleeing bomber, already eight miles away from ground zero. A shock wave, like a ring spreading outwards in a pond, suddenly shot skyward and slammed the bomber, buffeting it as if it had been hit by flak.

Below, the bomb, which had detonated at an altitude of 1,860 feet, had loosed a fireball 110 yards in diameter and a heat of 300,000 degrees centigrade. Granite melted. Roof tiles softened and changed color from black to olive or brown. People were vaporized, their outlines burned like negatives into roads, walls, and bridges.

The earth-shaking concussion flattened every building but those of the stoutest construction for two miles in any direction from the epicenter. Fires, hundreds of them, sprouted to life simultaneously and raged out of control until 4.7 miles of the city center had been incinerated.

The whirlwind unleashed by the blast tore trees out at the roots and obliterated walls, houses, and buildings. Trains, buses, and trams were picked up and thrown about like toys.

Minute crumbs of debris, thrown up into the atmosphere by the blast, fell earthward in a black sooty rain that left grease spots on clothes.

The sinister mushroom cloud climbed to 20,000 feet in sixty seconds. Then the spreading umbrella detached from its stem and floated upwards to 40,000 feet. From his tail gunner's position, Sergeant Caron could still see the ominous wreath when *Enola Gay* was 363 miles away. A tombstone of smoke that marked the death of Japan's eighth largest city.

For better or for worse, man had entered the Atomic Age.

Time has a habit of altering viewpoints, opinions, and beliefs. Causes for change can vary. They can range from new information recently brought to light; guilt feelings which prompt second guessing; or perhaps the previous mode of thinking upon which the opinion was based has suddenly become politically and even socially incorrect. It is even possible that alternative thinking could be the result of all the above. Perhaps this explains why after six decades, a sizable number of Americans are calling into question President Truman's decision to drop the atomic bombs on Japan. They argue that Japan was a nation against the ropes. That her ill-gotten empire had been wrested from her grasp.

That her once magnificent Combined Fleet lay rusting on the bottom of the Pacific. That her industry was in ruins. That food and other essentials were in grievously short supply. Some would even go so far to say that to resort to such a weapon against a nation in the throes of such disaster was a decision lacking in honor.

"After Pearl Harbor, Japan had no honor," remarked Harry Truman. If you were at Pearl Harbor that day or heard about the attack on radio or from family and friends, you might have been inclined to agree with the President. For Americans decades removed from the Day of Infamy, it is important for them to remember that the attack on the Pacific Fleet galvanized a pacifist nation looking to avoid war. That the attack was in direct contravention to the sense of decency and fair play that pervaded America at the time and which now seems to be a commodity in noticeably short supply.

As for the other reasons why the atomic bombs were dropped, these are based solely on logic. Yet still on the surface it all seemed pointless. For here was a small island nation, her naval power destroyed, industry shattered, without allies and friendless, fighting on against a worldwide coalition.

Any study of wartime Japan cannot be based solely on logic, at least not in the western sense. Pearl Harbor offers a prime example. While sneak attack had run counter to the basic American tenets of decency and fair play, to the Japanese it was an accepted practice. Surprise attack had been an accepted mode of warfare by the Samurai for centuries.

The Samurai spirit lived on in the Japanese soldier. He

was certainly one of the most courageous, yet reckless and fanatical of fighting men during the entire Second World War. To him surrender was unacceptable. Only victory brought honor to emperor, country, and family. The alternative was death, either in action against the enemy or by his own hand. This was the warrior code of Bushido.

Such was the code by which the Japanese militarists, in control of the education system, indoctrinated Japanese youth with the martial spirit and love of race. Not too unlike how the Hitler Youth prepared the young of Germany, but with a distinct Oriental flavor: *That the spiritual transcends the material.*

When the young recruit began his military service, he believed the opening line of his Imperial Manual: *Read this and the war is won!*

Just how much disregard the Japanese had for their opponents can be seen in their treatment of the enemy combatants they captured. Prisoners of war were viewed with brutal disdain, since they did not die in battle or kill themselves. Chinese POWs, in particular, were singled out for outrages of the utmost barbarism. Captured Americans, Britons, Australians, and New Zealanders fared little better. They were selected for such heartless indignities as starvation, disease, death marches, forced labor, massacres, and torture. Some were even killed and eaten by Japanese troops. By comparison, western POWs in the European Theater of Operations incurred a death rate of one percent at the hands of the Germans, whereas more than twenty-seven percent perished in Japanese captivity.

Of primary importance to the Japanese was the idea of

place. Japan was at the top of the hierarchy of nations. The emperor sat atop the Japanese caste system. He was not a man but a god. Detached from his people and accessible only to those privileged echelons of a stratified society. It was up to the military, the Japanese High Command, to run the Empire. And their doctrine was *Hakku Ichiu,* the Japanese version of *Lebensraum.* The militarists' agenda for conquest sought to evict the western colonialists and establish Japanese mastery over the Far East with a new order called the Greater East Asia Co-Prosperity Sphere. And the militarists did this by issuing directives in the emperor's name, whether he was aware of them or not. And what is more, dutiful Japanese believed and did what they were told.

Later in the war, when Radio Tokyo began to announce defeats, the Japanese were told that the High Command had expected such reversals, but that ultimate victory was assured. And the people believed it.

When the B-29s began to lay waste of Japanese cities with impunity, the Japanese people were told that the High Command had expected such attacks and were prepared to deal with the situation. And the people believed it.

Such was the grip that the militarists had on the Japanese people. A hold the High Command had no intention of relinquishing, even if it meant the wholesale destruction of Japan.

The terrain of Japan is not too unlike that of Okinawa. Much of it is a series of mountains, ridges, and forests from which a determined defender can exact a hefty price from an attacker.

Chairman of the Joint Chiefs of Staff, Admiral William D. Leahy, pointed out to President Truman that Army and Marine casualties on Okinawa had been thirty-five percent. He added that if the 767,000 troops earmarked for Operation Olympic, the invasion of southern Kyushu, incurred casualties at a comparable rate, losses would total some 268,000.

Truman was not about to let Japan become another Okinawa. On July 16, 1945, he arrived at Potsdam, Germany, for the Big Three conference with Winston Churchill and Joseph Stalin. That evening he received word of the successful detonation of a plutonium device at Alamogordo, New Mexico. The United States had the atomic bomb. Truman conferred with Churchill and Chiang Kai-shek of China. On July 26, the Potsdam Declaration was issued. Among the demands was that of unconditional surrender of the armed forces of Japan. That the Japanese people would not be enslaved or destroyed as a race (though war criminals would be subject to stern justice). That the new Japanese government would be based on such democratic ideals as freedom of speech, thought, and religion.

Many in the Japanese Foreign Office thought the demands stern but fair. This despite the fact that Secretary of State James Byrnes made no mention of the status of the emperor. But the Supreme Ruling Council, a collection of narrow-minded warmongers known as the Big Six, neither accepted nor rejected the terms. "*Mokusatsu*" was their reply. *Moku* meaning silence, and *satsu* meaning to kill. To kill with silence. In other words, Japan did absolutely nothing—except get ready for invasion.

The High Command's plan for the defense of the home islands was called Operation Decision (*Ketsu-Go*). Phase One entailed *kamikaze* attacks against the U.S. fleet and amphibious forces. These attacks would be mounted from air and sea. From October 1944 to August 1945, some 2,500 to 3,000 planes had been expended in kamikaze attacks. Yet the Japanese marshaled 5,350 planes for homeland kamikaze attacks with 7,000 more in storage and reserve.

The Imperial Navy scraped together 119 manned torpedoes and 273 midget submarines. In addition, 3,000 Shinyo motorboats were ready. Each was packed with upwards of two tons of TNT. Their suicide sailors would crash these into the sides of American warships and landing craft.

Phase Two encompassed the land fighting. The Imperial Army could field 2,350,000 troops. In addition, there were 4,000,000 Army and Navy civilians. A third force was also available: The Japanese People's Volunteer Corps. All men ages fifteen to sixty and women ages seventeen to forty-five were required to serve. It was reminiscent of Germany's *Volksturm,* and was a mammoth force of 28,000,000. They were to be armed with everything from bows and arrows and bird guns to knives, swords, and sharpened bamboo stakes. This was a nation set to commit national suicide. *Seppuku* on a scale so huge as to be incomprehensible.

On August 6, having received no reply from Tokyo to the surrender demands, the Americans dropped an atomic bomb on Hiroshima. The militarists attempted to downplay the tragedy, even going so far as to label the atomic bomb a mere four-ton blockbuster. This was later revised upwards to one hundred tons.

Emperor Hirohito took stock of Japan's deteriorating military situation. He ordered his foreign minister, Shigenori Togo, to inform General Suzuki of the Supreme Council that surrender was the only way left open to Japan.

General Suzuki called a meeting of the Supreme Council for 10:30 the next morning. The next morning, too, Nagasaki was vaporized; while on the Asian mainland, Stalin kept to the terms agreed to earlier in the year at Yalta. Three months after the surrender of Germany, the Soviet Union would go to war with Japan. Moscow unleashed its Far Eastern Army against the Kwantung Army in Manchuria.

Hirohito pressed his case for surrender. Yet the diehard militarists planned to resist. A group of officers went so far as to try and locate and destroy the emperor's recording of Japan's acceptance of the Potsdam terms. In this they failed. On August 15, Emperor Hirohito announced Japan's capitulation.

No other condition necessitated the atomic bombings of Hiroshima and Nagasaki than the masochistic obstinacy of the Japanese militarists. Only by direct intervention of the emperor was Tokyo spared a similar fate.

The question that comes up repeatedly is *did the bombs save more lives than they killed?* The answer is yes. Losses at Hiroshima and Nagasaki have been estimated as high as 200,000 to 300,000, which include those who succumbed years later to wounds and radiation poisoning. But an invasion of the home islands would have yielded many more Japanese dead. Also possible is that American losses would have been the heaviest ever incurred. The postwar estimate of a million American casualties may be debatable, but Leahy's claim of 268,000 certainly is not. Yet the admiral's projection was based solely on casualties expected from Operation Olympic in November 1945, and not Operation Coronet, the invasion of Honshu scheduled for March 1, 1946. And not included were the 100,000 Allied POWs still in Japan in August 1945. They were slated for extermination when the first Allied soldier set foot on the beaches. So a conservative estimate of 500,000 to 600,000 is not farfetched.

The claim that the decision to drop the bomb was a racist one has been given much credence. However, FDR wanted to drop one on the Nazis during the battle of the Bulge in December 1944. Of course the bomb was still months away from readiness.

Even before that, following the invasion of Normandy, Hitler was raining death and destruction on the British Isles with his V-1 and V-2 rockets. At one point, he was killing more civilians at home than soldiers in the field. Winston Churchill came under intense political pressure to address the situation. He gave serious consideration to sending clouds of RAF bombers to drench Germany in chemicals such as chlorine, phosgene, and mustard. Consideration was even given to using the Allies' most secret weapon after the atomic bomb, the N-bomb. This was an anthrax device, a hideous weapon that would have wrought unspeakable horror. Fortunately Roosevelt and Eisenhower talked the beleaguered prime minister out of resorting to such weaponry, especially since by that time, Allied forces were beginning to overrun the German rocket sites.

A comparison of the atomic bomb and the N-bomb deserves merit here. Just one atomic bomb caused unimaginable carnage and killed tens of thousands instantly. However, not so many years after their employment, Hiroshima and Nagasaki were rebuilt into thriving cities. Gruinard Island is a different story. The N-bomb did not have nearly the destructive capacity of "Fat Man" or "Little Boy." However, the contamination wrought by the anthrax bombs on Gruinard where they were tested rendered the island uninhabitable for more than forty years after the war. The rabbit population, nearly rendered extinct at one point, did come back, many with their coats of fur a different color. Only clad in a CBW suit was it possible to set foot on the island for decades after the war.

Not long after the Russians took Berlin, Averell Harriman toasted Stalin and the victorious Red Army at a dinner party. The stony-faced Soviet dictator seemed unmoved as he replied, "Czar Alexander made it to Paris." Thus the stage was set for the Cold War.

Of particular concern to Washington was that once the Soviets began operations in Manchuria against the Kwantung Army, they would gobble up enormous tracts of the Asian mainland. How much the Soviets gobbled up depended on how long it took for Japan to surrender. If Japan could resist for an extended period of time, then it would provide the Soviets with the opportunity to make Asia look like Central

Europe. A Soviet sphere of influence would face an Allied sphere of influence. The atomic bombings of Hiroshima and Nagasaki limited Soviet gains in Asia. This undoubtedly weighed in heavily in the decision to use the bombs.

It has been offered, too, that the United States initiated the nuclear arms race with the destruction of Hiroshima and Nagasaki. This is rubbish. That competition began in December 1938 when Otto Hahn and Fritz Strassman of Germany split the atom. Germany lost its initial lead in part because of the Nazi attempt to racially profile the science as "Jewish physics." Britain threw in its lot with the United States. The Manhattan Project was viewed by many of its participants as a race to achieve the bomb before the Germans. The idea of Hitler in the possession of such a weapon was unthinkable.

The destructive potential of atomic energy was not lost upon either the Soviet Union or Japan. The Soviets were able to explode a device in 1949 after the surreptitious assistance of Klaus Fuchs of the Manhattan Project. Japan was working on the atomic bomb as well. The Army and Navy each had its program. In fact the navy was working on a program of employing mini-atomic bombs on kamikaze planes. Of course this begs the question, did Truman know the Japanese were working on the atomic bomb? If he did, that would be almost certain reason to use it. But the fact of the matter is, whoever got it first undoubtedly would have used it.

The atomic bombs undoubtedly saved more lives than they

killed and brought a speedier end to the conflict. Yet there is another factor that must be taken into account when discussing the pros and cons of the atomic bombings of Hiroshima and Nagasaki. A factor that is just as important as any of the others that have been discussed; or maybe even more so. Yet it is rarely ever touched on. And just what might that be? Very simple. The bombs destroyed an idea.

The atomic bomb has been labeled many times as the ultimate weapon of war. Whether it is or not, it was the ultimate wartime product of an industrial system, a system the Japanese held in contempt. The atomic bomb broke the power of the Japanese militarists. And in so doing, it exposed a deity for what he really was: A man. The atomic bombs, then, saved the Japanese people from committing national suicide in reverence to an archaic and outmoded tradition.

And what of the bomb? Did it prove to be the ultimate weapon of war? No, as the superpowers found to their embarrassment in the rice patties of Southeast Asia and the rugged mountain wastes of Afghanistan. But out of the ashes of Hiroshima and Nagasaki, it did provide an uneasy peace and respite from global conflagration during the Cold War.

And what of myself? After all, I, too, am not immune from advancing my personal feelings on the subject. For after all that has been said and done, I do agree with the atomic bombings of Hiroshima and Nagasaki. For while I view the incineration of human beings as reprehensible, I feel somewhat relieved at the idea that this piece is not being written by a Japanese whose father sailed through the Golden Gate on the great battleship *Yamato*, through the human flotsam of burned and bloated citizens of San Francisco.

CHAPTER 5

Casus Belli

"In years hence and after all is said and done, history will not say that in 2003, Iraq attacked the United States." Mark Albertson

On March 19, 2003, the United States and Great Britain violated Iraqi sovereignty. In Blitzkrieg-like fashion, American and British forces routed an army of greater size, took Baghdad and Basra, and deposed Saddam Hussein. Yet the victory as touted by George W. Bush during his presidential grandstand play aboard the aircraft carrier *Abraham Lincoln* rang hollow. Remnants of Saddam's army, former Baathists, terrorists, religious fanatics, and a host of other malcontents struck back hard, tearing the prostrate nation asunder. Through it all, the question remains: Why the incursion in the first place?

During the 2004 presidential

campaign, the Bush camp routinely labeled Democratic challenger John Kerry as being inconsistent with his stands on the major issues. The catchphrase "Flip-Flop" became the Republican war chant, as they attempted to discredit their incumbent's opponent as being hopelessly indecisive. In fact, it was during the televised Republican convention that as Kerry's stands on the major issues were announced, the assembled throng shouted back to the rostrum in a chorus of "Flip-Flop! Flip-Flop!" with orchestrated regularity. Yet it is Flip-Flop that accurately describes the Bush administration's attempt to justify its unwarranted intrusion into Iraq.

The spurious justification for war began with the dissemination of the insidious fiction of collusion between Saddam Hussein and Osama bin Laden for the destruction of the Twin Towers in New York. Yet not one of the attackers was from Iraq. One was from Egypt. One hailed from Lebanon. Two were from the United Arab Emirates, while the remaining fifteen were from Saudi Arabia. It was two years and six days after the attack that President Bush finally admitted that no such intrigue ever existed.

The next bill-of-goods sold to the public and the press was the imminent threat posed by Saddam's "weapons of mass destruction." After years of UN inspections and more than five years of military occupation, this supposition has yet to be substantiated. Then came the swindle of bringing democracy to Iraq. Such was the mendacious litany of Flip-Flop espoused by the Bush administration for the invasion of a nation that had not attacked the United States.

However, for just a moment, let us not abandon the concept of a democratic Iraq. Such an idea is intriguing, though highly unlikely, at least as the concept is understood or practiced in the West. This is not to say that the order, independence, and liberation of the Iraqi people is an unworthy pursuit. Quite the contrary, it most certainly is not. But Washington did not undertake the Iraqi adventure for reasons so cavalier. Rather the underlying motive can be found in the words Order, Independence, and Liberation. The terms themselves are quite meaningless here. Rather it is the cryptic message that resides within them that is important. And the answer is easy to discern. Merely take the first letters from Order, Independence, and Liberation and spell it out... Oil.

As explained in chapter two, oil was the major reason for the liberation of Kuwait in 1991. And it provided one of the major catalysts for the aggrandizement of Iraq in 2003. This can be readily understood by consulting a map of the world.

First open your map and locate the Middle East. Begin by putting your finger on Saudi Arabia. Trace upward first to Kuwait, then on to Iraq. Finally run your finger to the right to Iran. You have just traced over four of the most strategically sought-after countries in the world. And why is that? Well, two-thirds of the world's proven oil reserves lie beneath the sand in these four countries. And that fact is based on U.S. government findings.

Oil, in one form or another, is in everything from aspirin to windshield wipers. It is the lifeblood of an industrialized power. The concept should be simple to understand: Without oil, America dies. And Yankee thirst for petroleum is unquenchable. The United States went from being a net exporter of crude, to requiring imports amounting to fifty percent of what it needs. This amounts to an addiction of twenty to twenty-five percent of the globe's daily output. And this from a nation that accounts for only five percent of the world's population. If this use of geography still has not clarified the picture, perhaps a sojourn into history will.

In 1945, Franklin D. Roosevelt brokered a deal with the Saudi royal family, which in essence amounted to U.S. military protection in exchange for privileged access to the kingdom's oil. Victory in World War II enabled Britain and the United States to tighten their grip on Middle East oil. But in 1953, a threat emerged when Iran's elected leader, Mohammad Mossadegh, nationalized Iran's oil to end long-standing British control. A coup backed by Britain and the United States saw the ouster of Mossadegh and the eventual installation of Shah Mohammad Reza Pahlavi to the Peacock Throne. British and American oil companies solidified their positions and Washington pumped in billions of dollars over the coming years to prop up the Shah's less-than-democratic regime.

In 1973, Israel, bouncing back from earlier reversals, defeated Egypt and Syria in the Yom Kippur War. Arab oil-producing nations retaliated by cutting oil exports to the West. Gas lines appeared. Streetlights, signs, and buildings were dimmed. Schools in some districts closed their doors to conserve heating oil. Again, in 1979, Iran shut the tap after the Iranian Revolution brought the world's first Islamic Fundamentalist regime to power. Gas lines reappeared and prices spiked.

It was clear that Western domination of Middle East oil

had come to an end. But this lesson in history was not heeded. The implementation of alternative sources of fuel, especially with regards to transportation, was not vigorously pursued, and in some cases, virtually suppressed by those whose special interests lay in jeopardy. In America, the gluttonous use of gas-guzzling vehicles continued unabated and was one of the major causes for Americans' increasing consumption of petroleum. Then in 1990, Saddam Hussein marched into Kuwait. The West countered this blatant aggression with a coalition of powers that included a number of Arab states. The coalition prevented the Iraqi strongman from doubling his reserves of petroleum, eliminated the threat he posed to Saudi Arabia, and thwarted his attempt to set the price of crude so as to be able to saddle his onerous debt from the Iran-Iraq War on the backs of his former benefactors. It also spawned a greater American military presence in the Middle East. A presence that afforded the more radical elements in the Arab world with the propaganda fodder necessary to cast America's growing presence as nothing more than Washington's attempt at hegemony. A new Crusade that saw the Arabs swap one colonial master for another. Only now the infidels were not their age-old antagonists from the Old World but an avaricious and impulsive state from the New. Regardless, they were still Caucasian and Christian. Yet these overseers practiced a brand of colonialism based not so much on armed force, as it was command and control forged on the purchasing power of a currency. A currency tied to the fossil fuel on which much of its value is based, and without which continued dominance of the viscous black gold might well begin the economic meltdown and military retreat of the globe's remaining super power.

This, then, calls into question the implied precedence of the War on Terror. Taking the fight to the terrorists was just another pretext trumpeted by the Bush administration for justification for an invasion of Iraq. Terrorism, though a dilemma, pales in comparison to Washington's goal of maintaining America's position as the world's leading economic power. Iraq is part and parcel of that strategy. And the war-torn country's importance to that strategy goes beyond the need for local control. And for clarification we need to return to our map.

Put your finger back on Iraq. Now move to the right until you find India and China. Since the collapse of the Soviet Union, these two up-and-coming powers are proving themselves able competitors. Their economies are growing at rates that approach double digits annually. They are making their presence felt in the global economy in such industries as autos, technology, and credit. In fact in 2007, China knocked Germany out of third spot in automobile production. The enormous populations of these two giants are demanding to enjoy the fruits of this boom. And such booming expansion is not possible without energy, and lots of it.

History shows that any nation that plans to enlarge its navy is seeking to project power and influence beyond its borders. Both India and China are buying and building larger fleets. For India, control of the Indian Ocean and Arabian Sea would allow Delhi to cut off Pakistan from the sea in time of crisis. It would also enable India to better protect its oil imports from the Middle East. With the appropriate amount of naval muscle, China would be able to threaten Taiwan, extend its reach into the Pacific, and vigorously press its claims for the Spratly Islands, which are believed to be home to massive deposits of oil and gas.

This will prompt Japan to reverse course and embark upon a naval construction program of her own. A resurgence of Japanese naval power will not set well in China and the Koreas, nations with long and bitter memories of brutal and predacious Japanese occupations. Russia, too, may consider Japanese naval expansion unsettling and be forced to take actions with regards to her strategic interests. Such a development will raise tensions throughout the Pacific Rim. Yet Japan imports every drop of oil and will be forced to take such actions, especially if Tokyo detects any flagging in American resolve.

But the threat from the east to American primacy is not coming just from the sea, but from land, too. The former Soviet client states of Kazakhstan, Kyrgyzstan, Tajikistan, Uzbekistan, and Turkmenistan have emerged from relative obscurity to undisguised strategic significance. These Central Asian republics are home to vast deposits of oil, natural gas, and desired minerals such as uranium and gold.

Following 9/11, the United States began to make inroads into Central Asia. American troops went into action against the Taliban and al-Qaeda in Afghanistan. U.S. military bases sprang up in Uzbekistan and Kyrgyzstan. Foreign aid was increased and there was even the hint of strategic alliances. But now U.S. influence is on the wane. Washington's focus on Iraq at the expense of Afghanistan has shown the limits of U.S. power. American support for the Color Revolutions in Georgia and Ukraine has warned Central Asian leaders that they could go the way of Eduard Shevardnadze and Leonid Kuchma. Indeed the fall of Askar Akayev during the Tulip Revolution in Kyrgyzstan in May 2005 was seen as part of Washington's "Freedom Agenda." Then there was the violent suppression in Andijan by Uzbek security forces, a crackdown that caused vigorous protests by the United States and the European Union. Tashkent ordered the U.S. to evacuate its military personnel and get out. This has allowed Russia and China to strengthen their positions in Central Asia.

The Shanghai Cooperation Organization consists of four Central Asian republics plus Russia and China. From the point of view of Moscow and Beijing, the idea of the SCO is quite simple: Advance the interests of Russia and China and shut out the United States. Russia is looking to strengthen its military ties in the region and attempt to get greater control of the republics' vast oil and gas deposits. The former would provide Moscow with a strategic success not seen since before the collapse of the Soviet Union, while the latter would give Russia more control over the energy supplies of the European Union. However, the EU is looking to circumvent the Russians by cutting its own deals with the Central Asia republics in the form of pipelines to the Caspian oil and gas fields.

Beijing, however, has taken a more subtle approach by attempting to control the Silk Road. Trucks head west daily loaded with vegetables, T-shirts, TVs, and all other manner of trade goods. China is building roads, laying tracks, and stringing pipelines. China's aim is to appeal to the Central Asian republics as a client and not as a rival. In this, Beijing hopes to undermine Moscow for control of the region, extend its political influence into such diplomatic hotspots as Pakistan and Iran, and isolate Washington from the region. This, then, makes the vast oil deposits in Iraq extremely important to the United States.

April 15, 2003, British Prime Minister Tony Blair, in an interview with *The Times,* stated, "Let me deal with the conspiracy theory that this somehow has to do with oil. There is no way whatever if oil were the issue that it would not be simple to cut a deal with Saddam."

Cut a deal with Saddam? In 1991, the industrialized nations banned together to evict the tinhorn dictator from Kuwait so as not to have to cut a deal. However, as history shows, Saddam was pretty adept at cutting his own deals. For instance, in 1971, Britain evacuated its forces from Kuwait and the Gulf States. In the post-colonial world, London could no longer afford to chase such global commitments and responsibilities. Saddam, forever on the lookout for weaknesses in allies or enemies, acted accordingly. The following year, he nationalized Iraq's oil.

The departure of British forces left a glaring vacuum, a vacuum Washington knew had to be filled right away. The question was, by whom? American forces were mired in the endless quagmire of Vietnam, while at the same time committed to the armed standoff with the Warsaw Pact in Europe. Israel, despite possessing the most competent military in the Middle East, was not politically expedient. So the nod went to the Shah of Iran. The despotic regent agreed to serve as Washington's proxy and guarantor of the status quo in the Middle East. As America's hired gun, the Shah was lavished with money and arms in exchange for his connivance.

When dealing with the Middle East, it is important to keep in mind that the Iranians are not Arabs, but Persians. Persians and Arabs have an antipathy that goes back centuries. Despite being an American tool, the Shah, nevertheless, began to meddle in the internal affairs of his Arab neighbor to the west, Iraq. Baghdad was having troubles of its own with its restive Kurdish minority in the north. The Shah kept stirring the pot by supplying arms to the Kurds. The situation finally proved untenable, and during the winter of 1973–74, hostilities broke out between Iraq and Iran.

Unlike its larger opponent, Iraq had neither the armed forces nor the foreign support for a protracted conflict. So Baghdad sought an accommodation with Tehran. On June 13, 1975, the Algiers Accords was signed by the belligerents. The Shah agreed to cut off supplies to the Kurds in northern Iraq. This enabled Baghdad to suppress the rebellion and restore order. But in return, Iraq had to relinquish claims to the disputed Iranian province of Khuzestan, known to the Arab world as Arabistan.

The Accords sought to end the dispute between Iran and Iraq over the Shatt-El-Arab waterway. This outlet is Iraq's only gateway to the Persian Gulf, and as such is extremely important to Baghdad's maritime trade, especially with the exportation of oil. The agreed upon demarcation line was drawn down the center of the Shatt-El-Arab. But it did little to improve Iraq's strategic position on the Persian Gulf.

Iran is blessed with over 1,200 miles of coastline along the Persian Gulf. At least five naval bases provided Tehran with a major maritime presence on one of the world's most important waterways. Iraq, on the other hand, is nearly landlocked. It enjoys maybe twenty-five miles of shoreline. Iraq had two naval bases squeezed into an area that amounted to not much more than a beachfront. And both were within range of Iranian artillery. Five years later, Saddam and his generals would try to grab more coastline at Iran's expense. In the meantime, events were moving quickly, events that were to radically alter the strategic complexion of the Middle East.

On January 26, 1979, the beleaguered Shah abdicated power in the face of the Iranian Revolution. In February, Ayatollah Ruhollah Khomeini returned from France after fifteen years in exile. He proclaimed Tehran as the capital of the world's first Islamic Fundamentalist regime. A regime that proclaimed itself an unflinching opponent of western domination of the Middle East, and a tireless foe of the United States, an infidel nation of godless values and reckless political and military ambitions. And it began its counter-reactionary agenda that November with the takeover of the American embassy in Tehran, in an effort to demonstrate America's impotence by tweaking the nose of the Christian superpower.

It was also during the fateful year of 1979 that Saddam

Hussein engineered a regime change in Baghdad. Like Joseph Stalin, Saddam ruthlessly purged those he considered a threat to his ambitions and tightened his grip on the reins of power. At the same time, the Ayatollah and his followers moved quickly. Like dedicated Trotskyites who were not content with merely consolidating their revolution at home, they actively sought to export their ideology abroad. They incited the Shia minority in the oil-producing province of Hasa in Saudi Arabia. Disturbances broke out in Kuwait and Bahrain. However, Tehran's main target was their gateway to the Middle East, Iraq.

Sixty percent of Iraq's population is Shia, a majority Muslim sect kept under thumb by the dominant Sunni minority. Tehran began its program of agitation by attempting to incite the Shias into overturning Sunni primacy. In March 1980, the Iranian government recalled its ambassador from Baghdad. The following month, Abdul Tariq Aziz, Iraq's Deputy Foreign Minister, escaped an Iranian assassination attempt, as did Iraq's Minister of Information, Latif Nusseif-al-Jasim. Border clashes soon broke out, and on September 17, Saddam renounced the Algiers Accords. Six days later, masses of Iraqi troops crossed over to the Iranian frontier.

Like George W. Bush, who prematurely claimed victory in Iraq in April 2003, Saddam told an Egyptian correspondent that the Iran-Iraq War would be over in three months. It would drag on for eight long, bloody years. And as the fighting raged, Iraq's fortunes began to flag.

In 1982, members of Saddam's inner circle—Baathist Party hacks, military officers, and members of his own family—offered Tehran a ceasefire. The overture was rebuffed. Infuriated, Saddam moved quickly to quell further plots by the schemers. He had many of the conspirators rounded up, then tortured and murdered. But what really saved Saddam were not his security forces, but America's aversion to the Islamic regime in Tehran.

Washington sent food, arms, and money to bolster the hard-pressed Iraqis. Satellite images of Iranian troop concentrations aided the Iraqi Army in countering Iranian attacks. But most important was the political recognition. Donald Rumsfeld, President Reagan's envoy, made several trips to Baghdad to demonstrate American solidarity. The Reagan administration did not want Iraq to lose as much as it did not want Iran to win the bloody contest. The Islamic fundamentalist government in Tehran would not be allowed to spread its gospel of revolution and reverse the status quo in the Middle East. This included turning a blind eye to Saddam's use of chemical weapons, even against his own Kurdish minority.

Iraq's use of chemical weapons offset the manpower advantage enjoyed by Iran. Many in Saddam's high command held the view that chemical weapons were no different than conventional arms such as planes, tanks, and artillery. The Iraqis began with simple tear gas and then upped the ante with mustard gas, Tabun, and cyanide. These and other agents were supplied by his western backers with the full understanding that their use was in direct contravention to the 1925 Geneva Protocol. But that made no difference.

Saddam Hussein was the new darling of the benefactors of Middle East oil. He was their new champion. The enforcer who would stop at nothing to counter the spread of the fundamentalist orthodoxy that threatened to tear apart the Sykes-Picot arrangement favored by the closed circle of opulent autocrats and their reactionary vendees.

But by 1990, Saddam had fallen from his exulted perch. He had grabbed Kuwait and attempted to extort his backers so as to be able to rid himself of his burdensome debt from his war with Iran. The U.S.-led coalition served him with his eviction notice in 1991. But he was allowed to languish because if his implied value as a bulwark against the fundamentalists in Tehran. This was the political price George H.W. Bush had to pay to get Arab nations on board the coalition so as to present the picture of resolute solidarity in the face of aggression.

Postwar Security Council Resolution 687 of 1991 mandated the elimination of Iraqi weapons of mass destruction and the facilities to produce and process them. In addition, no-fly zones were drawn upon the map of Iraq so that Saddam's warplanes could not strike the Kurds in the north and the Shias in the south. Iraqi assets overseas were frozen. Trade was curtailed, though some medicines and certain foodstuffs were permitted under the auspices of the Food for Oil Program.

Through it all, Saddam managed to survive. Many of his people starved during the embargo, but he and his followers did not. Nothing, it seemed, could bring about the wily dictator's downfall, except for maybe Saddam himself. For in 2000, Saddam mandated that Iraq's oil transactions no longer were to be based on the dollar, but on the euro.

The global oil market is based on the dollar. This fact

helps to keep the greenback as the world's reserve currency. Central banks around the globe keep ample supplies of dollars on hand to conduct their oil transactions. This affords the United States with distinct advantages. For many of these dollars find their way back to the States in the form of goods and services purchased. Many return when nations buy American certificates of deposit, treasury notes, or treasury bills, thereby financing much of America's ballooning debt.

Consider for just a moment the effects that would result if other nations decided to follow Saddam's lead. The value of the dollar would plummet. Prices of imports would soar. Declining interest in the dollar overseas would cause a financial crisis that would adversely affect the federal government's ability to afford Social Security, Medicare, Medicaid, education, defense, and so on. As the ranking global power, the U.S. needs to demonstrate that it still has the clout to keep its clients in line, even at the point of a gun. This can be seen in Iraq. For shortly after the invasion, Iraq's oil transactions were taken off the euro and put back on the dollar.

The United States has tightened its grip on Iraq with a string of military bases. There are 106 military facilities, and they range in size from small operating bases to facilities like Tallil Air Base. Tallil is an old Iraqi airdrome located some 200 miles southeast of Baghdad, not far from An Nasiriyah. Its two main runways stretch 9,700 to 12,000 feet, respectively. The base had fallen into disuse after 1991 when it was attacked during the Persian Gulf War. The task of revamping the area fell to the 407th Expeditionary Civil Engineer

Squadron. In the course of four months, the 407th hauled nearly 10,000 dump truck loads of dirt, dug trenches for more than 40,000 feet of cable, and embarked on more than 350,000 square feet of construction.

Another is Al Taqaddum Air Base. TQ is in the central part of the country some fifty miles west of the capital. It has two main runways of 12,000 and 13,000 feet. U.S. forces overran the base in 2003. Camp Ridgeway was soon established and became a hub base for the 82nd Airborne Division. The following year, Camp Ridgeway was renamed Camp Taqaddum. TQ also became an important staging area for Marine Corps Operations in Anbar Province. Leathernecks dedicated the airfield to Lt. Col. David S. Greene, a helicopter pilot with Marine Light Helicopter Squadron 775, who earlier in the year had been killed in action.

Another major base is Balad, located some forty-five miles north of Baghdad. It is served by two runways of 11,200 and 11,300 feet. Balad teems with all manner of aircraft ranging from unmanned Predator drones and helicopters to F-16 fighters and C-5 Galaxy transports. The base is one of the busiest in the world, moving five times the personnel in the course of one month than does the air base in Dover, Delaware. Balad's radar capability is extensive and can monitor the entire landmass of Iraq. The base can house upwards of twenty-five thousand personnel and provide them with all manner of Americana, including Burger King, Pizza Hut, and Subway.

Not far from Balad stands Camp Anaconda, a fifteen-square-mile facility that can house upwards of 20,000 troops. Camp Anaconda is not far from the eastern border of Dyala

Province, and so provides Washington with a powerful presence near the Iranian frontier.

However, no facility exemplifies Washington's aims for Iraq than the new United States embassy. This monument to American colonialism sprawls over 104 acres in Baghdad. Its size denotes its importance. As large as the Vatican, its twenty-one buildings are ringed in with blast walls fifteen feet thick. Upwards of 6,000 personnel can be accommodated, and they are right next door to the Iraqi parliament in the Green Zone. This location will serve to dispel any illusions held by the residents of Baghdad as to who actually runs their country.

The embassy was scheduled to open in July of 2007. This was changed to September. It has been subject to congressional investigations for such breaches of public trust as cost overruns, violations of building codes, and worker abuse. Just another in a long line of parsimonious outrages perpetrated by politically affiliated corporations in Iraq at the expense of the troops and the American taxpayer.

For those in the American electorate who believe their politicians who tell them that they will not rest until every American soldier is out of Iraq, think again. With the exception of maybe Ron Paul and Dennis Kucinich, none of the major candidates from the Democrat and Republican parties in the 2008 presidential sweepstakes had any real intentions of pulling all American troops out of Iraq for the foreseeable future. Why? Well for starters, why lay concrete for 12,000-foot runways and leave?

The United States has decided to establish its major military presence for the Middle East in Iraq. After six decades, Saudi Arabia has proven itself politically unreliable. The kingdom is home to Mecca and Medina, the holiest sites in Islam. Just the idea of masses of infidel soldiers in Saudi Arabia with their Burger Kings, rock music, and women soldiers in short sleeves and uncovered heads proved unacceptable to many of the faithful. It also provided a rallying cry for radicals such as Osama bin Laden, who likened the presence of American troops as a foreign occupation, reminiscent of the Crusades. Apparently many Saudis agree. For remember, most of the 9/11 attackers were Saudis. And Saudi Arabia supplies over fifty percent of the suicide bombers in Iraq.

Saddam's military weakness made him a ripe plum for the taking. By snagging Iraq, the United States served notice that it is no longer going to rely on proxies like the British, Kurds, or Shias; and neither was it going to farm out the duties of policeman of its interests to such transient despots like Shah Reza Pahlavi and Saddam Hussein. It has been fashionable to compare the conflict in Iraq to the war in Vietnam, offering the comparison that the Bush administration has mired the United States in another quagmire. However, on closer inspection it somewhat resembles Operation Just Cause in Panama. In Central America, the United States long relied on proxies like the Contras or paramilitary death squads like those in El Salvador to further its interests. But in Panama, Washington resorted to direct military intervention. Manuel Noriega, like Saddam Hussein, was just another sawdust Caesar who served U.S. interests. Thief, thug, and drug runner, Noriega was part of the illegal narcotics trade that helped to fund the activities of the Contras in Nicaragua. But when he outlived his usefulness to U.S. foreign policy, U.S. troops were sent in. Why U.S. troops? Because unlike other nations in Central America, Panama had a strategic asset too precious to be entrusted to proxies: The Canal.

Just like Panama, Iraq posed a tempting prize. In subduing Iraq, the United States has the opportunity to take advantage of the enormous amount of oil that lies beneath the sand. Second, it has served notice that the Almighty Dollar is still the world's reserve currency. Third, by taking Iraq, the United States has hemmed in Iran. Again consult your map. You will find American forces in Afghanistan, Turkey, Iraq, Qatar, and Bahrain. Fourth, from Iraq the United States can still perform its function of swing power in the Middle East as described in chapter two. And lastly and rarely mentioned in any discourse about Iraq is the emerging crisis posed by the dangerous lack of freshwater in the Middle East.

The population of the Middle East is about the same as the United States, some 280 to 300 million. This is about five percent of the world total. At current birth rates, the population of the Middle East is expected to double in less than twenty years. However, the region has barely one percent of the world's supply of freshwater.

Compared to many of her neighbors, Iraq is saturated. The plains and valleys of northeast Iraq enjoy annual rainfall in quantities that support the area's agriculture. Long-term concern here, though, is the deposits of groundwater. Though currently sufficient, they are nevertheless being depleted because natural recharge cannot keep pace with the demands of water use.

Iraq's other cultivated areas lie between the Tigris and Euphrates Rivers. These two waterways are recharged from melting snows and rain from eastern Turkey and northwest Iran. Flooding can at times pose a problem. And silt carried along the rivers poses a salinity issue in southern Iraq. Another problem is one that was manmade, and that was the wanton destruction of the marshlands by Saddam. The Iraqi strongman drained much of the area in an effort to punish the Shias living there. Estimates of the destruction run as high as ninety percent according to the U.S. Agency for International Aid.

However, water will prove to be as valuable an asset to the occupiers as oil. Water is important to the extraction of crude. Politically connected companies like Halliburton and Bechtel have the expertise to rebuild infrastructure so as to enable the United States to take advantage of Iraq's potential in oil and water; provided, of course, the country can be subjugated.

U.S. pacification of Iraq would bode well for Israel. At least fifty percent of the Jewish Homeland's fresh water comes from outside its borders. This is one of the reasons Israel will not give up the Golan Heights. Since the Golan watershed supplies northern Israel with much of its fresh water, any discussion of returning the Golan Heights to Syria must be accompanied by guarantees of fresh water. U.S. pacification of Iraq could solve that problem. It is certain as sunrise that Washington will make sure that Israel will get fresh water from Iraq. Indeed, control of fresh water in Iraq could very well turn out to be a major trump card for the United States.

Chapter 6

Decisive Front

On August 23, 1939, Soviet Deputy Minister of Foreign Affairs, V.P. Potemkin, waited at the Moscow Airport for Joachim von Ribbentrop, Foreign Minister of Nazi Germany. He warmly greeted the former champagne salesman and then whisked him away for a clandestine meeting at the Kremlin. Waiting to receive the emissary was Soviet strongman Joseph Stalin and his granite-faced foreign minister, Vyacheslav Molotov. They concluded what became known as the Nazi-Soviet Nonaggression Pact. Included were provisions governing the transfer of raw materials from the Soviet Union in exchange for manufactured goods from Germany. But more importantly the pact was a protocol establishing each signatory's sphere of influence. This included Poland. Hitler and Stalin did not merely intend to partition their neighbor, they meant to wipe the country off the map. The Germans would begin to close the vise on September 1, advancing east to Brest-Litovsk. The Soviets would close the eastern jaws on September 17 until Poland was gobbled up. As an added inducement for Stalin's compliance, Hitler agreed that Latvia, Lithuania, Estonia, and Bessarabia, which was on the eastern edge of Rumania, be included in the Soviet sphere of influence. The pact was signed at 2:00 a.m. on the 24th. The two dictators not only sealed Poland's fate, but jump-started the European civil war and set in motion a chain of events that would soon engulf the globe: The Second World War.

Bottles of champagne were opened to toast the historic moment. Stalin raised his glass to Hitler's health. "A fine fellow," remarked the Soviet dictator. Yet twenty-one months later the pact would prove to be just another scrap of paper. For Nazi Germany and the Soviet Union would collide in a titanic struggle that was to become the greatest land war in history.

In *Mein Kampf,* Adolf Hitler wrote, "State boundaries are made by man and changed by man…We National Socialists must hold unflinchingly to our aim in foreign policy, namely to secure for the German people the land and soil to which they are entitled on this earth…and turn our gaze toward the land in the East"

It is clear from the above passage that Adolf Hitler knew as far back as 1924, when serving time in Landsberg Prison for his part in the abortive Munich Putsch, that he would pursue the idea of *Lebensraum*—German expansion in the East. As he saw it, Germans had the right as the master race to usurp those territories rich in oil, wheat, timber, and livestock at the expense of those already living there. The inhabitants would be reduced in status to little better than slaves to serve their Teutonic masters.

Hitler's invasion of the Soviet Union, then, was the reason for war. From June 22, 1941, to May 7, 1945, the colossal struggle on the Eastern Front decided who was going to win the land war in World War II. By comparison, the fighting in North Africa was a sideshow. The invasion of Sicily and Italy, though important in opening the second front in Western Europe, was still a secondary front. Even the Normandy invasion and the subsequent advance across France, Holland, and Belgium still did not equal in size and scope the clash on the Eastern Front. This is borne out by some simple statistics. Hitler invaded the Soviet Union with 139 divisions, over seventy percent of Germany's available ground forces. By the end of 1942, German ground forces reached a peak of 262 divisions. Some eighty percent of this strength was committed to Russia. Even after the Normandy landings, at least sixty percent of the Wehrmacht was committed to the East.

Yet Hitler lost his bid to conquer the Soviet Union, and in so doing, condemned the Third Reich to a cataclysmic defeat. The question is, how and why?

During the 1930s, Hitler saw to the rebuilding of the German armed forces. By bluff, boast, and audacity, he marched into the Rhineland, Austria, the Sudetenland, followed by all of Czechoslovakia. But with the invasion of Poland, Britain and France at last gave up appeasement and decided to fight. The twenty-year hiatus of the European civil war had come to an end. Only now the leaders of the nations involved were no longer monarchs bent on trading a few provinces in exchange for continued existence. They were political realists like Hitler and Stalin, demagogues who settled for nothing less than moving in wholesale and achieving their aims by any means fair or foul. They proved the Treaty of Versailles to be a seriously flawed scrap of paper. They showed the promise of the Great War, the War to End All Wars, for what it really was: The cruelest hoax in the history of modern man.

Following the rape of Poland, the next seven months in Europe came to be known as the Phony War, or *Sitzkrieg*. This ended spectacularly in April 1940. Sitzkrieg gave way to Blitzkrieg, as Denmark, Norway, Belgium, and Holland fell to the overwhelming force of the Wehrmacht. And in a startling display of mobile warfare, the panzers humbled Germany's traditional foe, France, in just six weeks. By July, Hitler was at the pinnacle of his power. He held sway over an area that stretched from the North Cape to the Mediterranean Sea, and from the English Channel to Brest-Litovsk. Only Britain held out. And in her weakened condition, it was thought, that she, too, would soon be crushed by the Nazi juggernaut. But Hitler had other ideas.

In July 1940, Germany ruled the Continent. Yet it was an area devoid of many of the raw materials Hitler needed to maintain his Third Reich. One of these was oil. The Ploesti oil fields in Rumania were the only source of crude within his sphere of influence. Many raw materials such as oil were coming into Germany from the Soviet Union under the terms of the August 1939 Nonaggression Pact. But for how long? The Soviets in 1940 exercised their options in the pact to move into Lithuania, Latvia, and Estonia on the Baltic Sea. They also won territory from Finland in a four-month conflict, which ended in March. The Soviets gobbled up Bessarabia on the eastern end of Rumania. This put Russian tanks uncomfortably close to the Ploesti oil fields. With the Soviets on the Baltic Sea, Hitler's iron ore shipments from Scandinavia were now threatened. Therefore, at the end of July 1940, Hitler announced to his commanders his intention to destroy the Soviet Union.

Some of his commanders tried to dissuade the Fuhrer from such a venture. They argued that England was still not defeated. This meant that Germany would find itself in a two-front war, something which Hitler himself had written in *Mein Kampf* was a most grievous error. Nevertheless, Hitler countered, and with some merit, that even though Britain still held out, it was not a threat. So a rapid campaign in Russia would be the only active front. And the crushing defeat of Bolshevik Russia would show the recalcitrant British the futility of further resistance.

Hitler based much of his expectation on a quick campaign in the East on the Red Army's poor showing against the Finns during the Winter War. The Soviets attacked Finland in November 1939. A Finnish army of only nine divisions took advantage of the snow, lakes, and forests to inflict telling losses on the Red Army. Eventually the Soviets brought real weight to bear and defeated the valiant Finns. During the four-month conflict the Russians threw in upwards of a million men. Nearly 50,000 died, and more than 150,000 were wounded. It was believed in Berlin that this embarrassing performance was the result of Stalin's beheading of the Red Army during the purges of the late 1930s.

On December 1, 1934, Sergei Kirov was murdered. The popular member of the Moscow Politboro was also First Secretary of the Leningrad and Central Party Organizations. He was also viewed as a potential heir to Stalin. The assassin, Leonid Nikolayev, was shot. His wife, Milda Draule, was shot. The head of Kirov's bodyguard was shot. It has been alleged that Stalin rid himself of his most dangerous rival, then simply carried on from there. The party was purged of those who showed "deviationist" leanings, meaning anybody Stalin distrusted.

In 1937, the dictator started on his military. Marshal Mikhail Tukhachevski, a brilliant theorist of combined arms warfare, was implicated in treasonable activities on information supplied by Reinhard Heydrich's security service the SD. Whether bona fide or not, the unscrupulous Stalin needed little prompting. Tukhachevski was shot. And so continued the bloody harvest which saw three of five marshals, thirteen of fifteen army commanders, fifty-seven of eighty-five corps commanders, 110 of 195 division commanders, and 220 of 406 brigade commanders were all shot. Many of the survivors were sent to the gulags. Stalin's brutal heeling of the armed forces came at a frightful cost. The loss of experienced officers and their replacement by favored cronies showed itself in the Red Army's second-rate performance in Finland. Following the Winter War, reforms were immediately begun.

The Soviet officer corps enjoyed a rebirth. A cadre of officers, competent and tough, eventually emerged. Personalities who were to make their mark included Ivan Konev, later to be Marshal of the Soviet Union and a skilled practitioner of combined arms warfare; Vasili Chuikov, who made his name in the defense of Stalingrad; Paval Rotmistrov, the Soviet Union's acknowledged expert on armored warfare; Konstantin Rokossovski, twice a "Hero of the Soviet Union" and commander of the Central Front armies at Kursk, the greatest land-air battle in history.

Last but not least was Georgi Zhukov, Stalin's fireman, an abundantly talented commander who was instrumental in the defenses of Moscow, Leningrad, and Stalingrad. Zhukov first made his mark with Stalin with the defeat of Japanese forces at the Khalkin-Gol River in Mongolia, in June 1939. Zhukov had two qualities admired by Stalin: He was blunt in his remarks and, most important, he was nearly always right.

In July 1940, a little more than a month after the capitulation of France, planning began in Berlin for the invasion of the Soviet Union. On December 18, Hitler issued his famous Directive No. 21, Operation Barbarossa. The date to crush the Soviet Union was set for May 15, 1941. The Fuhrer would see to it that the German Reich would achieve *Lebensraum*. He would create his *Festung Europa,* or Fortress Europe, and its capital would be Berlin. For once the Soviet Union was smashed, the European civil war would be over, and the Thousand Year Reich would begin. Britain would see that help from the Soviet Union was not forthcoming, and that capitulation was the only course.

History tells us Hitler failed miserably. The question is, why? Some military analysts suggest that if Hitler had invaded on May 15 as originally planned, he would have had six more weeks of warm weather with which to work. But Italian bungling in the Balkans and British landings in Greece necessitated Hitler's response to protect his southern flank. This meant that the Germans had to subdue Yugoslavia, Greece, and Crete.

At the start of the Russian campaign, panzer commanders such as Heinz Guderian, formulator of Blitzkrieg, urged a drive straight to Moscow to cut the Soviet Union in two and destroy the city's political importance. But Hitler and some of his other generals, who were veterans of World War I and trained as infantrymen and artillerymen, seemed more intent in destroying Soviet armies in the field as opposed to occupying territory.

Following Army Group Center's spectacular victories at Minsk and Smolensk, Hitler siphoned off *Panzergruppe 3* and attached it to Army Group North for the attack on Leningrad. *Panzergruppe 2* and *Panzergruppe 1* were sent south to the Ukraine. Leningrad was not taken before winter, precipitating a siege that was to last more than 900 days and become one of the epic stories of the twentieth century.

Meanwhile in the south, Heinz Guderian's *Panzergruppe 2* and Ewald von Kleist's *Panzergruppe 1* conducted one of the greatest encirclements in military history and captured Kiev on September 16, 1941. The Wehrmacht bagged 665,000 prisoners, 3,718 guns, 884 tanks, and 3,000 vehicles. A grateful Fuhrer proclaimed Kiev as the greatest victory in the history of German arms. However, by the time Army Group Center was re-supplied and returned its panzer corps, it was October. The brutal Russian winter was in the offing. Temperatures soon plummeted ten, twenty, thirty, and even forty degrees below zero. Against such horrific conditions, the German troops had not been outfitted with the proper clothing or given the proper ointments and medicines to combat the cutting deepfreeze. German guns and vehicles lacked the proper oils and lubricants to operate in the biting cold. Some German soldiers had to cut sticks of butter with saws. Others saw their axes bounce off frozen horsemeat. In fact, so unbearably cruel were the arctic-like conditions that some who attempted to perform their bodily functions found that their anal pores had congealed, condemning them to a horrible death.

Nevertheless the Soviet situation at Moscow was critical. The heavy losses in men and equipment compelled Stalin to draw on a reserve he thought untouchable. His spy ring in Tokyo confirmed that Japanese eyes were firmly fixed on the Philippines, Malaya, and the Dutch East Indies. So for the defense of Moscow, General Zhukov brought in forty divisions of the Siberian Army. These were among the toughest troops in Russia and were trained to fight in winter conditions. On November 27, 1941, Zhukov unleashed his Siberians against Guderian's tired troops south of Moscow. On the nights of December 4 and 5, Zhukov counterattacked along other areas of the line. After getting close enough to see the spires of the Kremlin, the Germans were thrown back. German intelligence had not detected the existence of such numbers of Soviet troops. It was thought in Berlin that after such horrendous losses in the earlier battles that Moscow had no strategic reserves left.

By the end of February 1942, when the front had been stabilized, the Germans had incurred just over 1,000,000 casualties, including more than 200,000 dead, 725,000 wounded, and over 46,000 missing. The German army was out more than 2,300 tanks, 75,000 motor vehicles, 180,000 horses, 7,000 anti-tank guns, and nearly 2,000 artillery pieces. The Luftwaffe lost some 1,600 aircraft.

Soviet losses were more than 2,000,000 dead and wounded and over 4,000,000 captured. But Germany failed to win the quick victory so desired. And what is more, Japan had bombed Pearl Harbor, bringing the United States into the conflict. The European civil war had become a global struggle. And it would be a protracted conflict of attrition. Something Germany and her allies were unequipped to win.

Germany began the war without having mass-produced a long-range heavy bomber. The Luftwaffe, being a tactical air force, was given to support the army's swift-moving panzer spearheads as flying artillery. In the relatively short, sharp campaigns in the West, the strategic weakness of the Luftwaffe was not readily apparent. It became so during the battle of Britain. Aircraft such as the Heinkel He-111, Junkers Ju-88, and the Dornier Do-17 carried an insufficient bomb load and defensive armament to wage an effective strategic bombing campaign. This was again evident during the Russian campaign, when the Soviets moved much of their heavy industries east of the Ural Mountains. The Luftwaffe mirrored Germany itself: Unbeatable in a short war, susceptible to defeat in a protracted conflict.

Another German weakness was that of tank production. When the Wehrmacht invaded the Soviet Union, its panzer forces employed 3,580 tanks and self-propelled guns. At the time, the total world tank population was some 40,000 units. 22,700 of these were in the Soviet Union. Many were obsolescent types; however, the Soviets still enjoyed a six-to-one advantage. But just like in their attack in the West the summer before, the Germans employed their tanks in overwhelming strength at those points chosen for their armored spearheads; while the Russians, like the French before them, fed in their armor piecemeal or interspersed them into their infantry formations, thereby insuring their easy destruction by German tanks and anti-tank gunners.

But the Russians unleashed a nasty surprise in the form of the KV-1 heavy tank and the T-34 medium tank. At the onset of the conflict, the Soviets had only 393 of the former and 1,110 of the latter. These two tanks could outgun and take more punishment than any armored fighting vehicle the Germans could field. Of the pair, the T-34 would go on to prove itself the greatest all around tank on the Allied side in World War II. In fact it was the best tank in the world until the advent of the German Panther in 1943.

The T-34 mounted a high-velocity 76.2-millimeter gun, which was more powerful than any gun on any German tank in the early stages of the war. This was later replaced by the more deadly 85-millimeter weapon. The sides were sloped for optimum shell deflection, thereby eliminating the need for heavy slabs of armor. It was powered by a 500-horsepower diesel engine and had a top speed of thirty-four miles per hour. The T-34 had excellent cross-country characteristics. When German tanks became bogged down in the famed Russian quagmires, the T-34s with their wide nineteen-inch tracks kept going. The Soviets went on to produce more than 40,000 T-34s.

A weakness shared by both armies was that of motor transport. Germany invaded the Soviet Union with 600,000 motor vehicles. Many were of French and Czech manufacture, and therefore less robust than German types. Another drawback was the Soviet roads. Over ninety-five percent of Russian roads were not paved. This put a great strain on German mobility since the roads turned into quagmires after heavy rains or when the snows melted.

Another bottleneck was the railways. The Russian railroad system used a different gauge of tracking than their European counterparts. As the Germans advanced, the tracking had to be converted. This is why the Germans, like the Russians, relied heavily on horse-drawn transport. Germany began the invasion with nearly 625,000 horses. By the spring of 1942, nearly 200,000 German horses had succumbed to wounds, injuries, and disease. Many had been lost to the horrendous winter of 1941–42. At four degrees below zero, German horses began to freeze, and like the French and Czech trucks, proved less hardy than Russian horses. For instance, the Kirkhil ponies from Siberia, used by Cossack and Kalmuk cavalry, were able to withstand temperatures down to thirty degrees below zero. These rugged animals dragged guns and supplies over hills and through forests, lakes, and swamps. Of course Russian reliance on the horse was based on the fact that the Soviet Union did not have an automobile industry comparable to that of her western Allies, which retarded Soviet motor vehicle production. However, 475,000 motor vehicles were acquired by the Soviets through Lend-Lease. This was one of the decisive forms of assistance provided by Britain and the United States. Because as the Soviets learned the hard lessons of mobile warfare from the Germans, motor transport became a critical factor in the later stages of the war in moving supplies for the massive Soviet offensives.

Soviet motor transport was built on Lend-Lease. This is not the case with the tank. Just like the aircraft carrier was to controlling the vast stretches of the Central Pacific, the tank was essential to providing mobility and punch to the German and Soviet armies. Indeed it was the tank that held the key to the battlefield in the East. Germany produced 42,932 tanks, self-propelled and assault guns of all types. The Allies, through Lend-Lease, shipped more than 13,000 tanks to the USSR. Shipped were such models as the Matilda, Churchill and Valentine tanks from Britain, and the Lee, Stuart, Grant, and Sherman tanks from America. This was barely ten percent of Soviet production. And to a model were hopelessly inferior to such Russian types as the aforementioned T-34 and KV-1, as well as the KV-85 and the Joseph Stalin series of heavy tanks. This, of course, raises a significant point. From the latter part of 1942 on, the Germans were fighting on many fronts. The Russians were concentrated on a single front. It is indeed a tribute to the skill and daring of the German soldier that the war in the East lasted as long as it did.

A similar situation existed with regards to aircraft. The western Allies sent upwards of 14,000 aircraft to Russia. Unlike with the armored fighting vehicles, the Russians benefited from the receipt of some excellent American and British aircraft types. But again this was barely ten percent of Soviet production. And as the war dragged on, the Soviets fielded some marvelous combat aircraft such as the Lagg and Mig series of fighters. The IL-2 Shturmovik was more than a match for any ground attack and tank-busting aircraft produced by any of the belligerents during the entire war. And the Pe-2 proved an outstanding bomber, ground attack, and reconnaissance plane.

However, one glaring deficiency appears on the German side of the ledger, one which supercedes the quantitative and qualitative analysis of men, planes, tanks, and guns. It is often overlooked when measuring Hitler's failure in the East. And that is Hitler's racial policy. Adolf Hitler was a prisoner of his own virulent hatred of those he deemed as *untermensch*. He therefore condemned to failure his bid to defeat the Soviet Union before the first bomb was dropped.

Racial intolerance was a core belief of the National Socialist German Workers' Party. This racial intolerance extended beyond the hatred of Jews, gypsies, Slavs, Negroes, and others considered subhuman. Proof of an Aryan background was glorified by the Nazi Party. Verifying one's Germanness back to 1750 was one of the criteria for acceptance into the SS, Hitler's personal bodyguard which later grew in such dynamic proportions so as to become a state within a state. And this in a nation that had been one of Europe's most tolerant of its Jewish population. Countries in Eastern Europe such as Poland had dark records of pogroms and other forms of persecution. Germany, under the Nazis, took racial intolerance to new highs, utilizing German industriousness and efficiency to put together a system of ethnic cleansing and genocide, which continues to boggle the mind to this very day.

The Nazis' psychopathic desire to exterminate Jews, execute Communist Party officials and commissars, and subject Russian prisoners-of-war to the horrors of slave labor and countless other cruelties, turned a potentially friendly population into a decidedly hostile one. A populace subjected to the pitiless tyranny of Joseph Stalin might have been more receptive to a more benign German occupation. Areas such as Ukraine could have been accorded suzerainty under a German-dominated Europa. This would have almost certainly guaranteed a German victory in 1941 despite the brutal Russian winter.

But such thoughts were beyond Hitler, Goebbels, Himmler, and Heydrich. Such was their focus on racial purification that much time, manpower, and rolling stock were devoted to the monumental effort of transporting racial inferiors to the camps at the expense of the war effort.

Little wonder then that the U.S. Army Air Force, British Bomber Command, and the Soviet Air Force devoted so few resources to bomb the camps.

The conflict on the Eastern Front was the most determined land war yet waged. It decided which side was going to win the land war in World War II. The cost in human life was staggering. Eight to nine million died serving in the Soviet armed forces. Upwards of 13.7 million Soviet civilians lost their lives. The Germans lost two million dead in the armed forces. Another two million Germans lost their lives in the mass flight to the West in 1944–45. Approximately 25 million people died in the East. This is nearly half of all the deaths in World War II.

It is against such a backdrop that one can easily understand why the war was fought with such bitterness and savagery. For the war in the East was not simply a titanic clash between opposing armies. It was a war of German against Russian; Nazi against Communist; Hitler against Stalin. It is indeed the last named that largely accounts for the bestial manner in which the war was fought. Each dictator was as unscrupulous as the other. Each had no regard for his enemies and little for those of his own who slackened or faltered. Hitler's constant "Not a step back!" wasted many of the world's best soldiers, while Stalin had countless Red Army soldiers shot for cowardice by the NKVD or expended in his infamous penal battalions.

During the four-year war to the death on the Eastern Front, the Russians received mountains of food, medicine, clothes, radios, and raw materials from the United States and Britain. The merchant mariners and sailors who risked life and limb to deliver the goods are rarely remembered. The run to Murmansk was one of the most grueling of sea duties during the entire war. The valiant courage and skilled seamanship of the men who manned these ships must never be forgotten. But in the final analysis, the Russians defeated the Germans using Russian tactics, Russian organization, Russian weapons, Russian generalship, and most important, Russian manpower.

Chapter 7

America or Amerika

"This country, with its institutions, belongs to the people who inhabit it. Whenever they shall grow weary of the existing government, they can exercise their constitutional right of amending it, or their revolutionary right to dismember or overthrow it!" Abraham Lincoln

Before George W. Bush was sworn in as the forty-third president of the United States, sentiment had been building in the world community to relax the sanctions on Iraq. Washington and London were opposed to ending the embargo. And it is easy to see why. With sanctions lifted, Saddam would have been free to rebuild his shattered country. American and British firms would have been shut out of this massive reconstruction effort. Companies from France, Germany, Russia, China, Japan, and Brazil would have received lucrative contracts to rebuild Iraq. And despite

Baghdad's less than stellar credit standing, Saddam had more than enough collateral…oil.

Washington saw this as a strategic threat of the first magnitude. The Beltway brain trust was not about to cede six decades of hegemony in the most oil-soaked region of the globe. A worsening economic condition demanded that America take action to not only satisfy its energy requirements, but to preserve the privileged position of its currency…even if this meant military action. Subjugation of Iraq and control of its massive reserves of crude would not only salve America's energy demands, but would enable Washington to pump more oil into the world markets to undercut OPEC and drive down prices. At the same time, U.S. Navy control of the Persian Gulf would enable Washington to cut off adversaries from Middle East oil in times of crisis. But to accomplish this goal means the preservation of a geographical vestige of the bygone era of colonialism.

Iraq was the direct result of the colonial desires of imperialist powers eager to satisfy their insatiable appetite for aggrandizement at the expense of the indigenous peoples living there. And like America's current agenda, imperialist Britain forged the borders of Iraq for the very same reason, oil.

The Sykes-Picot Agreement of 1916 saw Britain and France greedily carve up the Middle East in expectation of the impending demise of the Ottoman Turks. Britain already controlled Persia and its oil that powered the Royal Navy. With Sykes-Picot, Britain could expand its Gulf holdings and extend its control over the region's vast potential for energy.

Penciled under direct British control were those areas of Iraq that extended from Basra in the south to just north of Baghdad and as far west as Karbala and Najaf. Those areas deemed under British influence included the important oil-producing region of Kirkuk in the north to as far south as the fringes of Arabia, then west across what is now Jordan and stretching across the Sinai to Egypt. The French zone of influence included portions of what is presently northern Iraq like Mosul, west to Syria. Under direct French control was much of Lebanon and modern-day Turkey. In reality, the scheming British saw their French allies as a buffer to the expansionist aims of Czarist Russia to the north.

However, London sought to revise its strategy when the Bolshevik Revolution toppled the Romanovs and knocked Russia out of the war. With the promise of oil in the area of Mosul, Britain decided to include this desirable piece of real estate in its zone of influence. Naturally this bit of duplicity upset the French. As a sop, London agreed to cut Paris in on a one-quarter interest in the British-controlled Iraq Petroleum Company.

The unfortunate Kurds were the big losers. When the British drew the borders of Iraq, they did so without regard for religious, tribal and clannish customs and traditions. The Treaty of Sevres did raise the prospect of an autonomous Kurdistan. But with British control of Mosul and the Turkish refusal to recognize an independent Kurdish state, the treaty became a dead issue. It was replaced by the Treaty of Lausanne in 1923, which recognized Turkey and relegated the Kurds to a status little better than that of a subservient people.

Arnold Wilson was Britain's procurator for Iraq. Wilson, a veteran soldier and administrator, had seen service for the Crown in India. Like the United States would later do with L. Paul Bremer, Wilson was to see to Iraq's colonization. Wilson, who later joined the British Fascist Party, found out quickly that this was easier said than done. Sunnis and Shias buried their differences and rose in revolt. When Wilson could not quell the insurgency, Sir Percy Cox was sent to replace him.

Cox began working with the Sunni Arabs in an effort to split his enemies. What he accomplished was the alienation of a disaffected Shia majority from any imposed government in Baghdad. The formulation of Iraq is quite typical of the post-World War I settlement at Versailles, where the victors redrew the map of the Continent to comply with their strategic agendas. However, a European-style settlement in the Middle East proved a precursor for disaster.

In Europe, the Hapsburgs presided over a three-ring circus of nationalism that made up the Austro-Hungarian Empire. But in the Middle East, the Ottoman Turks held sway over a dominion based on centuries of tribal, clannish, ethnic, and religious affiliations and traditions. The Ottomans more or less respected these differences. Islam was an integral part of Ottoman rule, where there was no separation between church and state. However, the Ottoman Empire failed to withstand the tidal wave of change unleashed by the cataclysm of world war. The victors, colonial powers from Europe, fashioned new borders to coincide with their strategic and economic agendas; a twentieth-century crusade that tore apart the ethno-religious fabric of the Middle East.

The European-style remapping of the region has resulted in ninety years of upheaval. And as long as fossil fuels are in demand, the region will be the target of domination or aggrandizement by global powers. For the present, the major protagonist is the United States. It seems that Washington's aim is to maintain some form of the colonial arrangement forged by Britain for the economic and strategic reasons previously discussed. And that translates into control of Iraq's oil and the preservation of the dollar. As long as crude remains the world's most traded commodity, and as long as it is important for the dollar to remain the world's reserve currency, the United States may be forced to engage in a more unilateral and belligerent foreign policy. Since America's dominance of the global economy is being successfully challenged, one way to maintain primacy is to exercise a controlling hand in the world's supply of energy.

Iraq, then, has no liberal-democratic tradition as in the West. Therefore, the application of American and European-style political and social mores into an area of tribal, clannish, and religious customs and traditions has little chance of success, especially when their application is effected under false pretenses. The objective of the Bush administration in 2003 was no different than that of Britain in 1920: Control of the region's oil. For if the main attraction were kumquats instead of crude, American troops would never have set foot in Iraq.

Following the conclusion of World War I, hope-filled people round the world came to see Woodrow Wilson's Fourteen Points as the promise of a New World Order, a world where nations large and small could determine their own futures free from foreign domination and encroachment. But the defeat of the Triple Alliance by the Triple Entente did nothing more than offer the victors the spoils of war. The imperialist agendas of Britain and France continued unabated. Old colonies were retained, and new territories were acquired at the expense of those living in Africa, Asia, and the Middle East. This sowed the seeds for future upheaval and conflict in such places as Iran, Iraq, China, and Vietnam. The global conflict fought by the succeeding generation was the tragic result of issues left unresolved by the conclusion of the Great War and the attendant collapse of the dynasties. It is abundantly clear that history shows quite tragically that scheming politicians always leave us with enough loose ends for another war to fight.

The United States emerged the victor in the decades-long Cold War. The Arsenal of Democracy and its allies had vanquished the last vestige of the twentieth century's totalitarian states looking to boss the world. Fascist Italy, militarist Japan, Nazi Germany, and finally the Soviet Union, all have been consigned to the trash heap of history.

However, the New World Order as espoused by George H.W. Bush proved illusory. The balance of power that had been buttressed by the spheres of influence of the globe's two major nuclear powers had suddenly lost its symmetry. The multilateral approach to security that proved successful in the standoff with the Warsaw Pact has been supplanted by an illiberal policy of unilateralism.

In 2003, Washington put this unilateral approach to security to work in Iraq. The Bush administration's sales pitch was the War on Terror, a distortion of the most impious hypocrisy. The United States overran Iraq because it had correctly assessed that the prostrate nation was weak militarily. The object of the exercise was to gain control of Iraq's oil and to preserve the dollar. As a declining power, the United States is reaching the point where American industrial and political clout no longer resonates with quite the degree of primacy that it once enjoyed around the world. The reliance on military power in Iraq may be a bitter portent of things to come. After all, the Bush agenda of unilateralism is another form of isolationism, codified and personified by the ominous collusion of monolithic government and corporate elite that surreptitiously circumvents the control and consent of the electorate. For the American people, in the end, do not elect their candidate for the nation's highest office. They go to the polls to cast their ballots for a pair of candidates selected for them by a two-party system backed by special interests. After all, can it honestly be believed that two political parties represent the wishes of 300,000,000 people?

The Nuremberg Trials showed that, in the end, the German people were responsible for the excesses of their leaders. And so it is with the American people. Not counting 2008, how many Americans have participated in the last several presidential elections? Just over fifty percent? France, which it is safe to say has not been one of the most popular countries stateside as of late, offers an example to aspire to. Of course, Americans will first have to get over their meaningless dilemma of french fries vs. freedom fries if they are to emulate the people who gave us the Statue of Liberty. For some eighty percent of the electorate went to the polls in the last presidential election in France.

But responsibility in a free society goes beyond the simple penciling in of a ballot on Election Day. Responsibility means attending common council meetings. Responsibility means answering the call for jury duty. Responsibility means calling, writing, or emailing your elected officials with your views. For there is no excuse for non-participation. It is the American people who, in the end, are responsible for the condition of this country. It is the American people who are accountable for the conduct of this nation, both domestically and abroad. The American people must realize that the checks and balances so carefully put in place by the founding fathers are there to prevent the usurpation of power by any of the branches of government. Those checks and balances are to preserve and protect the rights and liberties inherent in the Constitution.

The Constitution has been successful in curbing the excesses of the chief executive in the past. This is particularly true in the realm of domestic policy. Many inside government or from the business world, academia, and even private citizens for years have lent their talent, knowledge, and expertise to take action in support of or in opposition to initiatives put forth by the nation's chief executive. This has not been quite the case with regards to foreign policy. Here the majority of American citizenry do not have the expertise to question the aims of the president, or so they think. For most of the nineteenth century, the power of the president was limited because of America's preoccupation with domestic affairs; for example, the migration of pioneers across the virgin lands west of the Mississippi River. It is during the twentieth century that we see the rising power of the president, and this is due mainly to America's growing presence on the world stage.

The ascendant power of the presidency augurs an ominous course that the American people must address and reverse without delay. The prostitution of the War on Terror for territorial aggrandizement has cost this nation the moral high ground earned on September 11, 2001. Secret prisons, water boarding, Abu Ghraib, Guantanamo Bay, the Patriot Act, domestic eavesdropping all portend the coercive devices of the totalitarian state. And what of the vaunted press? Except for those islands of independent media and other uncompromising outlets in the popular press, compliant news trusts refused to ask the hard questions during the run up to the war in Iraq. Scripted press conferences with a president—who at times seems to have trouble putting together a pair of coherent sentences—is hardly flattering to the American people. The proper forum is for the press corps to ask the hard questions the American public needs the answers to if the masses are to decide to throw its support behind a leader bound and determined to take this nation down the most perilous path a president could ever embark upon: *war.* And as to whether it is appropriate to hold the chief executive accountable to public scrutiny during wartime, is certainly beyond question. And those members of the popular media like Bill O'Reilly who say they will spotlight such types as bad Americans seem to have forgotten what their proper function actually is. Such pronouncements from marionette pundits of corporate media differ little from the propagandistic bombast of such poisonous proselytizers as Joseph Goebbels and Julius Streicher.

America was formed on dissent, and dissent is just what is needed now as much as any time in our history. Where was the dissent when it became public that wounded American soldiers were found convalescing in a vermin-ridden fleabag hotel across the street from Walter Reed Hospital? So much for the "I Support the Troops" stickers on the back of every other Lexus, Infinity, Mercedes, and BMW you see. Where is the dissent against the obscene privatization of the war in Iraq, when the American taxpayer is getting his wallet picked to the tune of $99 per bag to launder the clothing of the troops? A well-known professional football player gets sentenced for organizing dogfights, while a member of the Bush administration literally gets a free ride for divulging the name of a CIA agent in time of war? Why aren't more of our elected officials upholding federal law and ruthlessly opposing the invasion by illegal immigrants? Why isn't Congress leaving no stone unturned to get to the bottom of the intelligence boondoggle that provided the pretext to attack a nation that did not attack the United States?

Domestic opposition to the war in Iraq has come in fits and starts, not at all reminiscent of the 1960s, when the raucous defiance to the war in Vietnam helped to bring down a president. However, you can rest assured that if a military draft were in place today, America's royalty would be out in force and at the forefront in organizing and underwriting the cost of an effective protest. But since when is freedom of speech and dissent the sole province of the well-heeled and politically connected?

Take the incident of well-known radio personality, Don Imus. His reference of "nappy headed hos" to a group of young black women was just another example of the crass humor typical of the modern-day shock-jock. However, Imus has a long history of poking fun at all colors, sizes, and types. But it is the witch-hunt begun by Reverend Al Sharpton that demands further scrutiny. This activist/cleric is a recognized champion of civil rights. But he is also a well-known personality in the Democratic Party, and his actions have to be judged in that light. For he knew his party had a good chance of taking control of Washington in 2009. So for possible consideration for a position in the new regime, it was certainly advantageous for him to remind the candidates and the electorate that he is still a champion of civil rights. But the American public needs no such reminders during an election season. It is quite simple. If you don't like Imus, shut him off. If you find Chris Rock's references to white people offensive, turn the dial. If you don't like Don Rickles, don't buy a ticket. The American public does not need to be told what it can or cannot listen to or watch, and should take with a grain of salt the actions of politically motivated clerics dressed in thousand-dollar suits and garnished in more jewelry than a display case at Van Cleef and Arpels.

After the colonies won their independence, George Washington found himself in a powerful position. He began the war with an army that was little better than an ill-equipped, ragtag band of farmers, cobblers, and blacksmiths. This armed mob soon coalesced into a potent force of guerrillas, which, in turn, evolved into a well-trained and well-led army. It was the classic example of taking armed citizens and molding them into a competent force for war as outlined years later by Mao Tse-tung in *On Guerrilla Warfare.*

But George Washington's greatest gift to America was not in organizing its first national army. It was not the defeat of the British. And it was not being elected as the nation's first president. When the Revolution ended, George Washington commanded a well-trained and battle-tested army, an army loyal to a commander-in-chief who had shared some of its trials and hardships. But unlike Julius Caesar, Napoleon Bonaparte, and other opportunists in history, George Washington did not make a grab for power. Instead, he went home. This rare moment in history allowed the embryonic colonies to form a nation and put into practice the laws, rights, and liberties put forth in the greatest documents for representative government in modern times. George Washington, then, began a tradition in America that has carried forth to the present day. It is called the *Peaceful Transfer of Power.* No other American in history has given this nation a greater gift. Not Thomas Jefferson. Not Abraham Lincoln. Not Franklin D. Roosevelt. Not Martin Luther King. The *Peaceful Transfer of Power* is the bestowment upon which everything else revolves. And we are in danger of losing it; or, more precisely, forfeiting it.

Tom Brokaw labeled those who answered the call in 1941 as the Greatest Generation. If they were the greatest, then America's revolutionary generation was certainly the most dynamic. But the priceless sacrifices made by the Dynamic Generation and the Greatest Generation to painstakingly mold and defend the rights and liberties that we hold most dear are in danger of having been made in vain. The greatest danger facing this nation is not radical Islamic terrorism as touted by Republican senator John McCain. America's growing inability to compete economically with the likes of India, China, Japan, and the EU is by far a much more pressing concern. And any aspirant for the White House who does not recognize this fact is not qualified to occupy the Oval Office. No, the greatest menace can be found permeating the vast stretches between Chesapeake Bay and the Golden Gate, and from the Canadian frontier down to the Rio Grande. It is the homegrown variety, that burgeoning vulnerability that results from the lethargy and antipathy of a disenfranchised electorate. A Maginot mentality that is engendered by the relentless dumbing down of the population as they are denuded of their rights and liberties by an unscrupulous clique of venal wealth, corporate elitism, and dissembling politicians.

A new generation of Americans, unswervingly loyal to the hallowed precepts of the Constitution, must rise to the occasion in the new millennium to confront and defeat the forces of arrogant greed, premeditated disparity, and perfidious ambition. In this they can expect no help. For their government has failed them. Their press has failed them. Big business has failed them. There is only one way for the American people to save this nation, and that is to take it back for themselves. When the American people realize that their obligation to this Republic is not limited to the parochial confines of the voting booth, then there will be change. When the American people demand a forthright and transparent accountability of the spending of public funds, then there will be change. When the American people demand the unvarnished and untainted reporting of events by their press, then there will be change. When the American people at long last realize that it is *they* who must protect the rights inherent in their Constitution, then there will be change. For the stark reality is, the rights and liberties inherent in the Constitution are guaranteed only if the American people are willing to make the commitment necessary to preserve them. The stakes are high, and the choice is clear. It is either *We the People* in America, or *We the State* in Amerika.

Sources & Postscript

On History: A Treatise was inspired to print only recently. Yet it has been a work in progress for many years. It is the fulfillment of much reading, writing and patient research. Chapters such as "Legacy of the Little Red Schoolhouse," "Swing Power," "Killers in the White Coats and "Genzai Bakudan" are elaborations of articles previously published in Connecticut newspapers. "Casus Belli," "Decisive Front" and "America or Amerika" were prepared especially for this work.

"Casus Belli" and "America or Amerika" are based on information gleaned and distilled from mountains of reports from such periodicals and dailies as the *Wall Street Journal, New York Times, Washington Post, Christian Science Monitor, U.S. News & World Report, Time* and *Newsweek*. Add to this political and history publications such as *Foreign Affairs, Foreign Policy* and *Current History;* defense industry magazines like *National Defense, Aviation Week and Space Technology, Sea Power* of the Navy League and the *Proceedings* of the United States Naval Institute.

The foreign press provided valuable information as well. *The Economist, The Guardian, The Times* and *Asia Times Online* just to name a few, offered sometimes a different perspective from the popular media stateside. A viewpoint that many times proved not only useful, but refreshing.

The internet offered a myriad of avenues for research. However one must be circumspect when sifting this smorgasbord of sources. For instance, among the sites I chose to make the most of were those of the United Nations, Central Intelligence Agency, U.S. Department of State and Department of Defense.

One site particularly useful was Global Security.org. It is a great source for obtaining information on U.S. military bases in Iraq and else where. Just type in "U.S. military bases in Iraq," and the listing for the web page for Global Security.org will appear. Click on it and you will find listed over 100 American military facilities in Iraq. Click on the name of a facility and an in-depth description appears.

However it is my belief that a greater understanding of the current situation in Iraq is lacking in much of the American electorate. For if such was not the case, opposition to the conflict would be that much more determined. For example, take the issue of "The Surge." First off, the term itself is nothing more than Madison Avenue mumbo-jumbo to gloss over the need for more troops. In World War I, an increase in troop strength was called reinforcements. So it was in World War II, Korea and Vietnam. But calling reinforcements in Iraq a surge lends legitimacy to a so-called change in strategy to deal with an evolving situation; when for all intents and purposes the Bush administration did not send in enough troops in the first place. But was The Surge the success the Bush administration touted it to be?

Well maybe The Surge's effectiveness can be answered by the Department of Defense. DOD released two maps on the sectarian make up of Baghdad. The first showed Baghdad at the start of the conflict, March 19, 2003. At that time, some 20 to 25 percent of the neighborhoods were Sunni. Another 20 percent were Shia. That meant that more than half the neighborhoods in the city were a mixed bag. The second map showed the sectarian make up of the capital by late 2007, when The Surge was deemed a success in putting an end to the civil war. By then 20 percent of the city was in Sunni hands. But the Shia controlled areas had blossomed to 60 to 65 percent; while the mixed enclaves had shriveled to about 10 to 15 percent. The question here is obvious: Was the Surge the success the Beltway blowhards claimed it to be? Or was it that the Shias won the battle of Baghdad? After all, they do control the government. And Shia militias staff most of the army and police. These are among the questions that American voters should be asking of their elected officials. But will they? Well if the plight of the wounded GIs who were left to languish in that run down hotel across the street from Walter Reed Hospital is any indication, the answer is probably no. Because if the American public truly cared about the well-being of those who don the uniform of this country to protect and defend the Constitution, then there should have been a outcry never heard before throughout the land…and there was not.

"Decisive Front" was written in an attempt to offer another analysis for Hitler's defeat in the East. It was also written to educate those who do not realize that the land war in World War II was decided on the Eastern Front.

The racial policy of the Third Reich as practiced in the Soviet Union was a despicable and shortsighted blunder. For it galvanized a population that might have joined in the quest to remove Stalin in the hopes of a better deal from Berlin. Still despite the horrors inflicted by the Germans, many people in the Soviet Union did cast their lot with the Nazis.

In 1942, the manpower squeeze was beginning to make itself felt with the Germans. Elements of the Cossacks, Latvians, Lithuanians, Ukrainians and Azerbaijanis were among the many ethnic groups who chose to serve their German masters. There were even volunteers from Stalin's home province of Georgia. By mid 1942, some 200,000 were serving behind the German lines in anti-partisan brigades, police battalions and other security units. By the beginning of 1943, upwards of one million Soviets were in uniform for the Germans. Some were transferred to France and fought the Allied landing forces on the beaches at Normandy on June 6, 1944. Soviet soldiers and civilians who threw their lot with the Nazi invaders is one of the more fascinating and unheralded stories of World War II.

On History: A Treatise never would have seen the light of day if it were not for many other works of history. Below is a roster of those which provided the greatest assistance.

Alperovitz, Gar, *Atomic Diplomacy: Hiroshima and Nagasaki,* Vintage Books, 1965

Ambrose, Stephen E., *Rise to Globalism: American Foreign Policy Since 1938,* Penguin Press, 1971

Baker, James and Hamilton, Lee, *The Iraq Study Group Report,* First Vintage Books, 2006

Bishop, Chris, SS: *Hitler's Foreign Divisions,* Amber Books, 2005

Brookhiser, Richard, *Founding Father, Rediscovering Washington,* The Free Press, 1996

Bullock, Alan, *Hitler: A Study in Tyranny,* Odhams Press Ltd., 1952

Burns, James MacGregor and Dunn, Susan, *George Washington,* Henry Holt & Co., 2004

Carell, Paul, *Hitler Moves East, 1941–1943,* Ballantine Books, 1963

Carell, Paul, *Scorched Earth,* Ballantine Books, 1966

Chaney, Otto Preston Jr., *Zhukov,* University of Oklahoma Press, 1971

Clark, Alan, *Barbarossa: The German-Russian Conflict, 1941–1945,* William Morrow & Co., 1965

Clark, Robin, *The Silent Weapons,* McKay, 1968

Congdon, Don, *Combat, The War With Japan,* Dell Publishing, 1962

Conot, Robert E., *Justice at Nuremberg,* Harper & Row, 1983

Conquest, Robert, *Stalin and the Kirov Murder,* Oxford University Press, 1989

Conquest, Robert, *The Great Terror,* Oxford University Press, 1990

Coox, Alvin, *Japan: The Final Agony,* Ballantine Books, 1970

Deutscher, Issac and King, David, *The Great Purges,* Basil Blackwell Publishers, 1984

Erickson, John, *The Road to Stalingrad,* Harper & Row, 1975

Erickson, John, *The Road to Berlin,* Westview Press, 1983

Etterlin, F.M. von Senger, *German Tanks of World War II,* Lionel Leventhal Ltd., 1969

Evans, Richard J., *The Coming of the Third Reich,* The Penguin Press, 2004

Evans, Richard J., *The Third Reich in Power,* Penguin Press, 2005

Friedlander, Henry, *The Origins of Nazi Genocide,* the University of North Carolina Press, 1995

Friedman, Norman, *Desert Victory,* Naval Institute Press, 1991

Gatzke, Hans, *European Diplomacy Between Two Wars, 1919–1939,* Quadrangle Books, 1972

Glantz, David and House, Jonathan M., *The Battle of Kursk,* University of Kansas, 1999

Glass, James M., *Life Unworthy of Life: Racial Phobia and Mass Murder in Germany,* Basic Books, 1997

Fugate, Bryan, *Operation Barbarossa,* Presidio, 1984

Goerlitz, Walter, *History of the German General Staff,* Praeger, Inc., 1957

Goldston, Robert, *The Road Between the Wars, 1918–1941,* the Dial Press, 1978

Grandin, Greg, *Empire's Workshop,* Henry Holt & Co., 2006

Guderian, General Heinz, *Panzer Leader,* Ballantine Books, 1957

Hale, Oron J., *1900–1914: The Great Illusion,* Harper & Row, 1971

Harris, Robert and Paxman, Jeremy, *A Higher Form of Killing,* Hill and Wang, 1982

Hart, Sir Basil Liddell, *The Red Army,* Harcourt, Brace & Co., 1956

Heiden, Konrad, *Der Fuehrer,* Houghton, Mifflin, 1944

Hersey, John, *Hiroshima,* Vintage Books, 1946

Hitler, Adolf, *Mein Kampf,* Houghton Mifflin, 1943

Hobsbawn, E.J., *The Age of Capital, 1848–1875,* Charles Scribner's Sons, 1975

Hobsbawn, E.J., *The Age of Revolution, 1789–1848,* Mentor Books, 1962

Hogg, Ian, *Gas,* Ballantine Books, 1975

Hohne, Heinz, *The Order of the Death's Head,* Penguin Books, 1966

Irving, David, *The German Atomic Bomb,* DaCapo Press, 1967

Jablonski, Edward, *Airwar: Outraged Skies/Wings of Fire,* Doubleday & Co., 1971

Karsh, Efraim, *The Iran-Iraq War, 1980–1988,* Osprey Publishing, 2002

Keegan, John, *The Iraq War,* Vintage Books, 2005

Kennan, George F., *The Fateful Alliance: France, Russia and the Coming of the First World War,* Pantheon Books, 1984

Kranzberg, Melvin, *1848: The Turning Point?* D.C. Heath & Co., 1959

Lafore, Laurence, *The Long Fuse,* T.B. Lippencott Co., 1965

Lefebure, Victor, *The Riddle of the Rhine,* E.P. Dutton, 1923

Lefebvre, Georges, *The Coming of the French Revolution,* Princeton University Press, 1947

Lefebvre, Georges, *The French Revolution,* Vol. I: *From its Origins to 1793,* translated By Elizabeth Moss Evans, Columbia University Press, 1962

Lefebvre, Georges, *The French Revolution,* Vol. II: *From 1793 to 1799,* translated by John Hall Stewart and James Friguglietti, Columbia University Press, 1964

Leonhard, Wolfgang, *Betrayal: The Hitler-Stalin Pact of 1939,* St. Martin's Press, 1986

Lewis, Bernard, *What Went Wrong? Western Impact and Middle Eastern Response,* Oxford University Press, 2002

Lukacs, John, *June 1941, Hitler and Stalin,* Yale University Press, 2006

Lifton, Robert Jay, *The Nazi Doctors,* Basic Books, 1986

Macksey, Major Kenneth J., *Panzer Division, The Mailed Fist,* Ballantine Books, 1968

MacMillan, Margaret, *Paris 1919,* Random House, 2001

Mao Tse-tung, *On Guerrilla Warfare,* Praeger Publishers, 1961

Massie, Robert K., *Dreadnought: Britain and Germany and the Coming of the Great War,* Random House, 1991

Marx, Joseph Laurence, *Nagasaki: The Necessary Bomb,* the MacMillan Co., 1971

May, Arthur J., *The Age of Metternich, 1814–1848,* Holt, Rinehart & Winston, 1967

Mee, Charles L., Jr., *The End of Order: Versailles 1919,* E.P. Dutton, 1980

Mellenthin, Major-General F.W. von, *Panzer Battles,* University of Oklahoma Press, 1956

Milsom, John, *Russian Tanks, 1900–1970,* Galahad Books, 1970

Nafziger, George F., *The German Order of Battle: Waffen SS and Other Units in World War II,* Combined Publishing, 2001

Orgill, Dennis, *T-34, Russian Armor,* Ballantine Books, 1971

Piekalkiewicz, Janusz, *Moscow, 1941,* Arms & Armour Press, 1981

Polk, William R., *Understanding Iraq,* Harper Collins, 2005

Proctor, Robert N., *Racial Hygiene: Medicine Under the Nazis,* Harvard University Press, 1988

Rashid, Ahmed, *Jihad: The Rise of Militant Islam in Central Asia,* Yale University Press, 2002

Rashid, Ahmed, *Taliban,* Yale University Press, 2002

Reitlinger, Gerald, *The SS: Alibi of a Nation, 1922–1945,* Arms and Armour Press, 1981

Remak, Joachim, *The Origins of World War I,* the Dryden Press, 1967

Ricks, Thomas E., *Fiasco, The American Military Adventure in Iraq,* Penguin Press, 2006

Ritter, Scott, *Endgame: Solving the Iraq Crisis,* Simon & Schuster, 1999

Roraback, Amanda, *Iran in a Nutshell,* Enisen Publishing and Nutshell Notes, LLC, 2006

Rose, Steven, *CBW: Chemical and Biological Warfare,* Beacon Press, 1968

Schlesinger, Arthur M., Jr., *War and the American Presidency,* W.W. Norton & Co., 2004

Seagrave, Sterling, *Yellow Rain,* M.Evans & Co., 1981

Shikara, Ahmed Abdul Razzaq, *Iraqi Politics, 1921–41,* LAAM Ltd., 1987

Shirer, William L., *The Rise and Fall of the Third Reich,* Simon & Schuster, 1959

Shlaim, Avi, *War and Peace in the Middle East,* Penguin Books, 1995

Talmon, J.L., *Romanticism and Revolt, Europe 1815–1848,* Harcourt, Brace & World, 1967

Taylor, A.J.P., *From Sarajevo to Potsdam,* Harcourt, Brace & World, 1965

Taylor, A.J.P., *The Origins of the Second World War,* Atheneum, 1961

Taylor, Edmund, *The Fall of Dynasties,* Doubleday, 1963

Thomas, Gordon and Watts, Max Morgan, *Ruin From the Air,* Scarborough House, 1977

Thompson, David, *World History, 1914–1961,* Oxford University Press, 1964

Toland, John, *Adolf Hitler,* 2 Vols., Random House, 1970

Toland, John, *The Rising Sun,* Vol. 2, *The Decline and Fall of the Japanese Empire, 1936–1945,* Random House, 1970

Watson, Bruce W., George, Bruce, MP, Tsouras, Peter and

Cyr, C.L., *Military Lessons of the Gulf War*, Greenhill Books, 1991

Weiss, John, *Ideology of Death: Why the Holocaust Happened in Germany*, Elephant Paperbacks, 1996

Werth, Alexander, *Russia at War, 1941–1945*, Carroll & Graf Publishers, 1964

Wilcox, Robert K., *Japan's Secret War*, William Morrow & Co., 1985

Wyden, Peter, *Day One: Before Hiroshima and After*, Werner Books, 1985

e|LIVE

listen|imagine|view|experience

AUDIO BOOK DOWNLOAD INCLUDED WITH THIS BOOK!

In your hands you hold a complete digital entertainment package. Besides purchasing the paper version of this book, this book includes a free download of the audio version of this book. Simply use the code listed below when visiting our website. Once downloaded to your computer, you can listen to the book through your computer's speakers, burn it to an audio CD or save the file to your portable music device (such as Apple's popular iPod) and listen on the go!

How to get your free audio book digital download:

1. Visit www.tatepublishing.com and click on the e|LIVE logo on the home page.
2. Enter the following coupon code:
   2270-fc83-615f-38fc-d1d4-f3b4-27df-feb9
   Download the audio book from your e|LIVE digital locker and begin enjoying your new digital entertainment package today!